The Adventure

The Adventure

Frederick Pollack

Story Line Press | *Pasadena, CA*

The Adventure
Copyright © 1986, 2022 by Frederick Pollack
All Rights Reserved

No part of this book may be used or reproduced in any manner whatsoever without the prior written permission of both the publisher and the copyright owner.

ISBN 978-1-58654-367-9 (tradepaper)
    978-1-58654-111-8 (casebound)

The National Endowment for the Arts, the Los Angeles County Arts Commission, the Ahmanson Foundation, the Dwight Stuart Youth Fund, the Max Factor Family Foundation, the Pasadena Tournament of Roses Foundation, the Pasadena Arts & Culture Commission and the City of Pasadena Cultural Affairs Division, the City of Los Angeles Department of Cultural Affairs, the Audrey & Sydney Irmas Charitable Foundation, the Kinder Morgan Foundation, the Meta & George Rosenberg Foundation, the Allergan Foundation, the Riordan Foundation, Amazon Literary Partnership, and the Mara W. Breech Foundation partially support Red Hen Press.

Second Edition
Published by Story Line Press
an imprint of Red Hen Press
www.redhen.org

Contents

1 ☘ 11

2 ☘ 91

3 ☘ 181

Author's Note

This poem was written in 1981–82 and first published in 1986. Some of its attitudes are as dated as its technology. I'm still proud of it.

... somehow assured of escape.
—Auden

1

The dead feel

shock
as if caught
in some dreadful indiscretion. And while I

didn't have to remember
anything, and so didn't,
grief

underlay everything. And that one duty
I still cannot define.
Yet I thought,

accept this and go mad
for eternity. Or sane . . . but mad or sane
it will be for eternity; you should

keep your options open. I became
superficial.
I awoke. The forest was full of life.

Beetles and spiders, and that
part of a bird's time
spent on ground. Ant columns

avoided me, worms twitched away.
Broad brown leaves, moist, softened twigs.
I was neither warm nor cold.

Sedate, wide-scattered
elms and maples
and an opossum

mother and young, moving among the weeds.
Ground mist.
Other animals stared. I was

playing for millennia
with the snooz-alarm, long past that job
or any other demanding

awakening. Soon would put on
a woodsman's stance, his open balancing hands,
an explorer's,

a survivor's measured glance—as if
familiar. Meanwhile I dozed.
The sense

of having once been tucked in
prevailed. I sought it
like a beloved

sleeping face,
a face sleep captured
halfway to a smile.

                    Walked, then,
out on the lower slopes.
Valley ahead. Behind, above the elms,

birches and alders;
pines above those, rubble,
sheer cliff

of pink and grey
granite, snow-topped. White
stags moved up there.

The mist lifted.
The valley was so vast
that I felt

replaced. Meadows, more forests,
water,
distant snowy peaks. I hadn't

expected this again, reconciled to
crowds, privacy
a moment in an elevator.—No sign

of people. No
need, I thought, still sleep-confused.
A breeze

lackadaisically brought
the smell of pines,
then of fruit,

bland, yet
exciting once: butterscotch, vanilla, an intense
tapioca. It

clustered under the boughs
of low-spreading trees
at the forest margin. Dun, gourdlike—I

shied back: a
breastfruit? Was there an implied
insult? I glanced around.

Why not. It smelled good,
I trusted it. Light,
easily peeled; meat of a pear, a cheromoya,

and at their heart I found
seeds smaller than an apple's—the merest hint
of star-shaped seeds.

                Birds called
from points separated
by so much empty air

                      that, straightening,
I felt sudden
joy . . . there was something.

I had come through.
All this was mine.
              The fruit

seemed so bland, I recalled
steak: the "Ben Jonson's"
in San Francisco. Had taken Susan

(with Jack's permission) in '70 . . . '71,
on a dare: "If you just put on something"
beside that stained blue shift

she lived in, smoking
Marlboro Hundreds to the bone, "you'd be foxy."
"Like a real woman.

Oh. I'm sorry. You were being complimentary,
weren't you. I didn't need to
ideologize. I don't even feel—" "Look.

Wear something else and I'll
take you to the Ben Jonson's." So she sewed
an ill-fitting dress. The breastfruit

became drier,
saltier, and as I focused:
smoky, gravy-moist. That's easy,

I told myself: enzymes in the pulp
pick up the changes in my saliva.
Hint of dessert.

A bite of wine. Pleased, I
hefted the thing,
pushed

towards others
through the last green, the first yellow
grass. Rills

gushed from outcrops
towards the central stream. I knelt and drank.
The legendary purity.

      Behind the trees,
animals
just out of sight. Part of a fox.

The smell of
something circling, watching,
only professionally afraid. Someone

else tracked droppings
to a burrow; patrolled.
I drank blood.

The dead fat
haunch, afterwards, a favorite
momentary rest.

Or resting with her
and the kids
between needs, vaguely playing,

observing my digestion,
then dragging myself up. Sometimes
friends

romped
onto the yellow grass,
testing safety, barking,

snapping each other's throats, never caught. Until,
tired of weight
I flew

out and over, following the stream,
the southern thermals,
the bits and specks

of high-flying food; settling
as light failed,
on the home-bough, to make my report.

And lick my fur
in a clearing absolutely mine, considering
and removing

the day-spoor. To wash
and share
the evening fish, from the high creek,

noting the last
rustlings, snappings,
sighings . . . as the king

climbed home. Stern, sometimes
playful, kind to his own;
tracing late smells

for miles against the simple background
of pine and ozone—
until the cowering one

was visible, even
to my dim eyes . . .
                Only time

remained,
and me not knowing.
If I kept on,

I thought, I would become
one of them. Only one—
to hunt, or scavenge

to the woods' end, and be
alive again?
an animal—So I returned. Glad,

however, to have won through
to them. The technique
might prove useful

later, if I
came back this way.
                Dusk,

smooth purple
broken by shapes and cold. Somewhat
lost in myself

I didn't want
night. Sank
against a tree and closed my eyes,

only a moment, exhausted;
the fruit fell from my hands.
Day. Downslope,

richer flowers
than the white woods-iris.
My shoes cut

the only path, and I sweated.
And poked thoughtfully
through the musty

turtleneck (the type one wore
in cafes, in
the glory days,

to make one merely massive). Given my success
with the breastfruit, maybe—
here—I thought,

I can
change. Focused
sudden frenzied hatred

on various lumps, and they dwindled. I knew what
muscles would feel like:
the little messages,

the excitement. New
veins throbbed. I tensed
my belly, and it stayed tensed.

I flexed my biceps
and they sucked
mass from the under-wattle. Peculiar

balloonlike feeling; then, power. Living
ghosts jumped
from weeds being trampled, I kicked

and kicked at them. Hair, sharp
sight, hearing
came back

at half a mental glance. A certain
arrogance.
By the time I reached the stream I was a muscleman.

Extreme. I slackened
slightly . . . weeping with effort and joy.
                                            A butterfly

rose from the grass—
a stranger,
surely, to this

climate? Big,
fiesta-colored,
nature's attempt at insignia. And filmy green

bugs, more interested in flying
than biting. Irises,
snapdragons, wild

roses thronged the banks, old willows trailed.
Things turned
white in the distance.

A herd of... something grazed
downstream. No young among them.
No bulls upslope. I checked. No watchful

mother. One
waited, nibbling
flowers and weeds

as I approached
(holding my baggy trousers). It turned
to face me and I laughed:

no more a horse
than a man in a horse-suit. Not a cow
or a bear, though big and solid, a child's

drawing of an animal.
Absurd the huge sad eyes,
the wide hand-puppet mouth

dribbling greens. The legs crude pillars,
the hooves (—what?
elephant stumps) hidden

in fur. The fur warm
grey, blue-tinted,
springy ringlets. No fleas

leaped from my touch, no flies circled.
I scratched it
between the ears. It lowered its head.

I scratched its silly face
at which I could not stop smiling. It
stuck out a wide pink tongue

and rasped
my lean new bicep.
                    I mounted

gracelessly (had never done this). It
emitted a dying-fall sound
between a whoof and a whinney

and started
after its vanished friends. I scanned the hills.
There, above the breastfruit,

elms and pines,
stood the larger
animals I had been.

Above them,
caves. I had fated
myself to caves, once. They would be

an ideal house from childhood (not
a model of a world
but a world built to my scale.)

They would contain
danger, (1 would want
danger, eventually.) And where there is danger,

I thought cloudily, safety must be. The highest
cave would contain
the skull of a bear.

                            The beast moved slowly.
"I'll name you Juggernaut,"
I said. He twitched

a stubby ear. When
I half-heartedly
kicked him, he gave that

moan again, and I accepted
something absolute
about his pace. His back was really too broad,

broader than a horse's
as I understood it. I sat cross-legged,
wondering how I looked. A

pasha in a howdah,
silly and giggling. I doffed my shirt,
stroked

myself. Then, yielding to it,
I lay on my back
on his back. Smell, texture of

deep-pile carpet
beside plate-glass windows
long ago, sunwarmed.

I squinted against the light.
                              Creek noise.
Ducks. A sudden

flight. Catkins,
pussywillows
patrolled and occupied

by red-winged blackbirds
guarding the essential elegance.
There had been

someplace like this; of course
not quite so vast
nor I so alone. (Was I

disappointed? Anything
determinate would be
disappointing, and this fact in itself

wasn't, and the reality of this place
not too pronounced.)
      Quail, fleeing.

When the creek
widened, wood-strewn
beaches formed, and little islands where

... *ouzels* hopped. A
catkin of some sort?
broke in the middle; wherever it touched

water, the water foamed ...
I sat up,
tugged Juggernaut's ear.

He stopped. It
was soap. I submerged
noisily. Birds

protested, scattered. The seed-pod
was rough. l drew it
over my clothes,

gingerly over my
steel stomach, defined arms,
butt solid as bone. My cock—

an extra, this, not
consciously demanded: noticeably larger. I
dived, swam

(weeds and ooze
down there, one feeding duck). Splashed
Juggernaut, who looked

away, licking drops. I laughed and sang
the Ode to Joy,
pummeled myself. No fat met my fingers.

I stopped.
It might come back
if sought. Glee

became forced . . . as if
I had always been
like this, without noticing.

          It was evening
when I met
somebody. "Evening" in that

the light sank,
evenly, from everything.
I had poised

my hand over
Juggernaut's back, over the boles
of trees we passed, to catch

that bit of darkness.
                    I wasn't ready,
wasn't

talking to myself yet. Given
time, I could have
rehearsed

how it was to happen.
What I would say, what he or
she would say. What we would wear:

A judge's gown. Ceremonial robes.
He was standing
on the south bank (if

the river flowed west,
as I believed
without evidence). He was not facing

us. I nudged
Juggernaut in. Waves
swirled about my legs.

                        He stood
mid-meadow. The glint
of the spike

of his umbrella had
originally caught my eye. I wished
suddenly that twenty forests,

a hundred mountain ranges had
hidden him, but then,
of course, I would have missed

something.
                    Black male,
white-templed; neat

derby with grey band
black morning coat, checked slacks
straw had settled on.

He held the umbrella
tightly rolled, under his arm.
—Face small, lips tight, eyes

closed. I saw him peek
and breathe, and
when we did not leave,

tremble. He was short.
From where 1 sat
                I could have kicked his face in.

I asked him something . . . Felt
tired. One had to work,
I thought, even here—differently,

under better conditions, but still
work. (As we rode
off, I wondered

what I meant.)
The white
of his eye, receding . . . Was it his

landscape, I merely
his devil?
1 considered, angrily rejected this.

                      Now I saw
signs, subtle and half-absorbed,
of man. A path

too wide for deer. A rock
placed on another, as if
someone had started

then lost interest in
that religion. Which is silly,
I thought, men don't build dolmens

from faith, but to
work off potlatch. Do I know
what I'm talking about.

Juggernaut found some berries.
I eyed them, shrugged.—Unfilling. Vile,
intolerable

that hunger should arise
under the steel-plate
muscles. The fact

of night
bothered me now, but I wouldn't
wish this one away.

A fine rain fell.
                The meadow ended.
Trees closed in, the land rose. Don't

catch cold, I told myself. Plan
for next time.
The animals

had walked their circles
into the grass and folded their paws.
A housecat

lurked between roots . . . did you wander
away from your mistress and die
and keep on wandering? "Disgusting

weather, isn't it." He
fled. An owl
swept so near

I heard his wings
flap. No
moon. Typical. If

worse came to worst, I could sleep
beside Juggernaut, if
we found a cave.

If his legs folded.
                                        We reached
a hillside clearing, and a shrine

and a big man
glimpsed between pillars.
A sculpture. I walked

up the low, unswept steps. The head
deeply bowed, hands
dangling between knees. The face in shadow

in whatever light.
                                      Lehmbruck's "Seated Youth."
The bronze felt very cold,

the stone base, less.
I sat and shivered. Should bring
Juggernaut in.

No. The columns,
the roof, carved wood. Deep reds
predominated, probably. Some

gold. A late
expressionist, Jugendstil. Plant forms, yet
straightened, as if

men had invented them.
                         Too dark
to read the words,

if any, along the eaves. I thought of Lehmbruck,
suicide in '19. A "generous"
suicide . . . we lack terms

to discriminate this: the deaths of others
had hurt him.
                         Shouldn't there be

a candle? My
conditioning hadn't
prepared me for shrines.

Or vigils. I heard
Juggernaut
munching his way uphill. The storm,

a shifting probing
din. Really I wouldn't have
                         kicked him in the face.

Possible
confused percussion of horsemen
amidst the rain, their voices

the usual hostility,
balked.
Living out silly Conan fantasies.

I didn't look
although 1 wasn't hiding. Only
wished I were sure

they knew I was in here
and that the shrine had power.
—Mould, vine smell. The

wind. I
glanced up at him
occasionally, was touching him

when lightning flashed.
I thought of losses,
then, very delicately, a loved,

a hated face.
Contemplated
my own cold, marble arm. This

in some sense is for me,
I thought. Though I had been
no longer young. What

am I supposed to feel?
I felt.
      At dawn

the mud
may have looked trampled.
Sore and pleased

I called Juggernaut, not caring
if they were still around. He hove in view,
fluffy and snorting,

eager, perhaps, to be gone. Ignoring hunger,
I kept the swollen river
in sight, below. Rapids,

a considerable falls. After some miles
I remembered I
hadn't read the inscriptions.

Composed some.
                    Saw the house
early, but arrived

only at dusk. Juggernaut wouldn't be hurried.
Nor would I. All
morning I rehearsed

wise
people, a battle
of ego versus abstract

ego for
trophies of self-respect. I
urged Juggernaut higher,

seeking a general view. The house—
palace, rather—commanded
a break in the mountains. Beyond,

plains stretched
endlessly south
into haze. The pools, lawns,

fountains, formal gardens,
beautiful, correct, confident,
were a shock

as the temple in the rain
had not been. For hours
among the trees, it was lost to sight.

Then we picknicked, my
steed and I. Breastfruit seemed
rare on this bank.

He found roots.
I picked berries, amused myself
tossing them to him. He

snuffled, sedately
cavorted after them.
I told him stories.

Yet as night fell
I abandoned pretense, and hurried.
         Light

streamed from french windows
across the lawn. It was assumed
that one would cross the lawn.

        I left Juggernaut
at the edge of the forest.
Regretted

the lack of a tether, then thought
better: he
should have his freedom.

He was unfit
to canter along the
great curved drive, be reined in

before the distant, canopied
main door—and I dismount
with a single leap

and flourish of my cape, my hat, my plume,
if I had a cape
or could ride. Music

among the lights:
Tippett, possibly,
Rawsthorne, Maw? The door

of this minor east-side entrance
opened, and a girl
in maid's costume

twittered beside me. A string quartet,
I gathered, and a clarinetist
just arrived from the City. Monsieur had missed

the singer. Monsieur was late. I can't
appear like this, I whispered,
smiling frantically

back at her. I had to change.
I needed a bath.
Surely they had

something to change to? "Mais,
bien sûr!" And she tugged me
through a Georgian,

magazine-strewn hall, up a staircase. A
powder-room door
opened, below us; a strong old man

in full dress uniform
inspected me. I learned
later that from vanity

or lethargy he had
retained his ancient kidneys.
This wasn't

the grand staircase. She led me there
along a spacious corridor,
then up. I liked the light

in this place, an endlessly reverberated
cool passionless white. She
talked without stop,

unassimilable goodies: indeed,
Monsieur was expected.
It *was* Rawsthorne. Clothes . . .

she unconsciously
wrinkled her nose
at what I wore: one cannot dream

to be issued much better
upon awakening. And those soap plants
were "méchant,"

"inéfficient!" I had stopped
longer than expected
that morning "au sculpture Laim-brouck." (I was sad

she didn't call it a shrine.) "I'm not
used to *tubs*" I said,
"places I lived

mostly just had showers
and if there was a tub
well I'd

try to keep it clean
but the walls behind it
were usually disintegrating... but here, of course,

I'm sure it's a lot nicer—" "Oh!"
yes, it was: sunken,
terrazzo tile, 40 square feet

without the jacuzzi.—Not
vulgar, more
a kind of positivism... the fun of describing

replaced that of having? Her little
black-clad butt
switching back and forth; the red smile

awkwardly over her shoulder
at me, lumbering along behind (I needn't
lumber, now), fired me. I

would shake the house
with the great club of the bed. She would break windows
with her screams, I with my roaring.

I undressed
in the bathroom (really a room,
larger than anyplace); handed my

clothes out,
carefully, through
a crack in the door. Then floated

full-length amidst bubbles.
From here I couldn't
hear the string quartet. Only her singing

some lively Canteloube air
of peasant love, meanwhile
turning down sheets,

arranging flowers
in silver vases
on the low table, the high

mahogany desk. I wanted to linger
in the bath, but not so long
that she lost

the pretext of working.
I regarded
my lean length, still city-pale.

Not long enough in the wilderness.
Tried to perfect,
hone the new thing,

define my
arms and thighs still more, and
lay my own ghost . . . was that

a phrase, here? It must be
a familiar experience.
There were towels,

rich and green, but no robe.
I stepped out.
She hovered, holding the robe—

the one thing she had forgotten—
averting her eyes. "Ah non, monsieur, non
je le veux bien, mais

je dois attendre là-bas." But I didn't
want her to attend. She undressed quickly
to get it over, then

for another reason. Her nails
trembled on the snaps
of the black garterbelt. I no longer

needed the crooning pleading
spilling from my mouth. She flung back
the covers, lay

across the bed. Seemed not to know
what to do with her arms
and legs, thrashing. Her cunt glistened. I

threw myself on her.
                              Towards dawn I did
a trick with time, so that we lay

days together,
feeling no other hunger
and sleeping

intermittently. Merely touching
her breasts awhile made her come,
and I moved

my tongue for hours
between her inner lips. We
bathed in that tub,

laughed about bodies,
talked about France,
sex, food, avoiding

other topics. The uniform,
whatever it meant, gathered
dust on a chair. I liked

keeping her from
her duties, knowing that no one
dared knock. One feels

(she said)
special, naked. Then in the
moonless overcast nights,

listening to the rain, or enjoying
the moist breeze
from the south, I watched her sleep:

damp
shadows at
armpit and groin, her breasts

pressed to my side,
things I had deserved.
      I wanted

to wake her, saying, Hey,
we've come through, we've
really put one over,

haven't we? All of us,
the other guests
you denied for my sake, the Countess—(thus

she had referred
to her boss). She,
Yvette, smiled, still

bright and alive
in sleep; making an occasional
moue at a dream.

          I dreamed
that the concert
had gone unusually well, even

for that noted group: the clarinetist
(an unsuccessful
Berlin Wall crossing) smiled

via eyebrows. The young Welsh
violist (car wreck), whose "Nocturne"
came later, ran easily

through the unrewarding chromatics
of his part,
          happy about

something in the City. (Both violinists were
older men, late of the New York Pro Musica.) The cellist,
a lambent norvégienne, whose career

had only begun here, drew
unprecedented beauty
from her solo

in the adagio, regarding
the hostess
with frank desire . . . their

gowns as white as the room. It was a dream
like the piece in it, an
elegy. The Countess

smiled, responding. The General
checked his
uniform for drifting specks, was

also immensely pleased.
The painter
slouched motionless, dark glasses

held by the chandelier.
        I also dreamed
that when I descended,

leaving Yvette asleep, the music stands,
wineglasses, the painter's
half-empty Fritos bag

remained. I was disturbed
the place hadn't been cleaned up. My
fault, I realized.—I had missed the party. Realized

it had been for me.
        When I awoke
she was gone, and I dressed

in kid boots, tight breeches, Byron shirt,
a hip-length cape.
The salon

was clean, aired. (Household
robots? other staff? or
were things simply clean

when they should be?) It spread
from chaise to sofa,
end-table to writing-desk, hedged

by vases
of flowers. Books,
good ones, yet

with an undemanding air
of resort-hotel flotsam.
                        Someone was reading Turgenev.

Five big
Abstract Expressionist canvases hung
in french-window light. Kline-

derived, inconclusive; strong
in context.
                        It was a woman's room.

A tall stooped stork
stood in a corner
communing with an ashtray.

Pale, bald young, narrow-
lapeled black suit, black narrow tie.
Those shades.

(When he took them off,
close-set eyes
guarded the beak.) "Smoke?"

                              he asked.
     "I was trying to quit..."
                           "That doesn't matter

here. You cancel out
things."
              "I've noticed that,"

I said, accepting
a gold-tipped Sobranie.
                           "Yeah...

you can wait
till your lungs rot, and the docs
are growing tissue on your

shoulder for a
tracheoplasty—sort of
playing chicken, you know. Then you focus

in on it, and really
want it to go away,
and it does. Suddenly your

throat's back, and your lungs, you
take a deep breath... Fans say
there's nothing like it." "I did something

similar, with my belly—" I
began, but he
disliked

the elegiac tone;
oozed from the room. Who the hell
is he? Which of us

is dominant?
I wondered. Stood
straighter, arranged my cape. In this

graceful room, in this female palace,
I was the honored guest
                                  but followed

into the kitchen
where gadgets gleamed
on miles of counter. Slowly and evenly

he spread peanut butter
on a slice of dark rye
on a delft plate

                        then, deliberately, abandoned
knife, crumbs, loaf,
jar, and leaned

on the counter, facing me and eating
without discernible joy. (I
watched, fascinated. He had

                                lived on peanut butter
on Second Avenue, watching
McCarthy from barstools, dying

before McCarthy. A
disease, probably. Slow, without
visions. Or pity,

except from his family,
wanly
waving, as it were, from

as far as possible. Yet he felt
that their lives, at least,
grew ... accumulated towards

some sort of fulfillment. Pity
also, from girls he had lived on
—to buy paint, doubtless; meanwhile

lifting
caviar, pate, pickled-pigs'-feet from
the little groceries. That sense of

everything available somewhere
forestalled resentment. The
big dreamy cars

he parked all winter
midtown had
warmth in them. Some changed hands.

Things changed hands
in them, in a vast
unseen realm. Other

scams: the college boy,
deliveries,
elevators, dope. Sometimes

Mingus insulting crowds
at the Blue Note insulted
him. Desmond's, Tristano's

ice became
the one "honest" sound, he insisted. Talking
as one talked as

corner-of-mouth
apodictics gave way
to wonder, analysis,

trailing off, whining. Dylan's
grin
warmed him one afternoon

at Julius', was withdrawn. Sometimes he sat
cross-legged, and stared
at a candle—but it became

the flame of memory,
the flame of lust, the atom bomb, never
nothing, and the girl

watched, shivering. Friday
lectures on 8th Street, some clarity. One
question, for years: if it comes

out of the collective unconscious, how much
is *mine*?
is *me*? Galleries

effusive, inconclusive,
gone. One group show.
But Kline,

Kline especially, at the Cedar Tavern—that rumbling
masculinity. Never
one word addressed; the great

jokes retailed. The L,
his brown walls
trembling. Rats. Before it came on

he though he would see
night in Sao Paulo. Fights in Ceuta.
Whores in Rotterdam. The sea. Better

even to polish doorknobs
on some aircraft carrier in
the Gulf of Japan

than this life. Toward the end,
a strange
wish to go back

to something like Newman's or Rothko's
late-surrealist flower-pieces: not yet
the farewell to things, but

the moment of takeoff.
                            Or so I imagined.)
"Yeah, it's

a tricky technique, that editing. Like I say
you gotta focus
in on something. Like you were praying.

Different, though. Praying
don't work. I prayed. This is
                            will. Will creates

everything, here." He
stopped chewing his sandwich.
"The Will to Power

you know. Like in Nietzsche.
The unaided power of the mind." "Do people die here?"
I asked, opening the fridge. The fridge

was a dream: shirred eggs, pressed
duck, pâté, quiche, flan, mousse,
all in perfect order. "It's difficult,"

he said. For the first time
now, his pallid grin. "Your instincts
save you. You slip

in the shower, you get a . . .
instant replay." He savored the phrase. "It's
what old Yvette

is doing right now."
                                                       "Doing."
"Editing. What I call editing. Or will

if she's Late. She wouldn't
want to be Late."
                                    "Are you jealous?"

I asked, eating. He grinned,
poured
coffee from the samovar. "Those paintings out there

are mine," he said. "The Countess
supports young talent." "You are
from the Fifties, then? I wasn't sure

if your outfit meant
Fifties, or its 'punk' imitation."
                                            "What sort of outfit

are you wearing?" he asked,
                                  split. I
still felt unequal;

followed him
into the foyer. Yvette,
in a one-piece green

swimsuit, carrying
suntan lotion and towels, held
black, very brief trunks

out to me. (The older man
I had seen also stood by.)
I approached,

took her in my arms,
demonstrating
something; feared

she would pull away. But she gave
the kiss
the time and tongue it required (though

eager to swim, I thought.) The feel
of her suit, her flesh beneath . . .
                                    Then we walked

as if onto a stage
down to the terrace, past it, to the pool.
Beyond the cabanas,

bar and deckchairs,
lay the Gardens
and the plains—perhaps literally endless—

(what one could see
through the mountain gap)
                                  dotted

with herds
of something. I
remembered silly Juggernaut. The scented

air . . . I changed
in a cabana. Why
suits, I wondered, decided I knew.

                                    Yvette
swam, but still found time—or
it was the afternoon

in the form of some genial spirit, who put
drinks on the bar, and
in the little depressions

of our chairs. Then she rode,
squealing, the high corkscrew
waterslide. The painter found

a polarized facemask, and
a snorkel, and flailed
the length of the pool, then slid

into a floating chair
and drifted, drinking.
                        The Countess

sunbathed, framed by
mountains and sky. In that light
her gold hair

shone, her skin
gleamed. As I
slowly, formally

neared, she
extended her hand, and
it was as if

the horizon touched me.
                                        Her calm face.
"You're my hostess,"

I said. "I've selfishly
enjoyed all this, these last . . .
Forgive me for not—" "No need

to apologize. You're welcome here."
                                       Her voice. "Please,
don't get up." "I won't.

I'm resting now.
We'll talk later." She turned
on her belly, unlacing the tie

of her cream-colored
top. "It's odd
about the light," the old man

sitting nearby spoke. "There is no sun,
only a certain
direction one cannot face." "Sure I can,"

I countered, his
pleasant tone grating
worse than the painter's claws. "*Try*,"

he urged. I raised my head
toward a certain quarter of the heavens,
but could not look . . . "Yet her ladyship

will tan, yet
there are no shadows, only
an homogenized twilight. I miss the sun,"

he said. The breeze
lifted white hair
from his brow. He smiled at something

ahead of him, and a little below. "We also
haven't been introduced." The thick-veined grip
was not strong.

Desert shorts,
loose shirt ... "Don't you plan
to swim?" "Not really,"

he said. But I did,
and made
        a spectacle on the high board,

then played tag
with Yvette, chased her
into a blue-tiled bay.

We hugged the wall. She,
coolly: "No more
shy boyish kisses like

the first last night
now you have meet
ma patronne? I have—how you say—

outlive my usefulness!" I took in
the Countess' back, the thoughtful
General ... the painter

paddling with one foot,
                        and a mood
remembered from my whole life

rose. "Hell, no," I growled,
swept her
toward me, feeling

two men's eyes.
                              Fried chicken
had appeared, hot buttered rolls

in a basket with a red-and-white checked
cloth. Dripping, I
piled high a paper plate, left

white meat for the complaining
painter,
        wandered

into the Garden, far enough
that the near calm
prevailing round the pool

gave way to wind. In my mind,
the line of the Countess' back;
the glorious Nordic,

somehow begging forgiveness yet
always already forgiven, and
loved

instantly.
                Walls
of flowers

surrounded me,
bowing: trumpetvines,
hibiscus, highlights of

wisteria
        and roses,
including the black one. Sudden teasing perspectives

between the rows.—Talking,
I thought, through scent.—No,
why. No need. And if

the few remaining ambiguities
prove insuperable
I could do worse

than sign up
with these ... Mirrors,
after all, were still showing

what mirrors had always shown, my
mother trying to become my father
                                  but these

flowers
so surrounded me, I felt stronger
in that soft earth

than in any woman's arms; until
on a far crest
I saw the horsemen.

                Stood
wondering what to fear. What violence
horsemen might mean, and I deserve.

Wished them away. They
didn't go away,
except in their own time.—Real

horses. I resolved
to mention them to the General. But in
so big a Garden

they were forgettable.
                        He had gone in, and the Countess.
Yvette and the painter

laughed, splashed. As dinner neared,
mistress and maid vanished.
One dressed

for dinner, here. Wanted to,
perhaps for the first time. The General
shone,

    transformed from
the eternal pensioner of
poolside. Somewhere among the sunbursts

and crosses
some pip
indicated Retirement. I

wore burgundy, and
another black cape. The painter
did not change. We

took cognac
in a green
and shimmering silver

Art-Deco drawing room
only sketchily feminine. A big grey cat
occupied my lap and purred.

                        "Why do you think
there's no sun?"—the General,
erect in his armchair, "if I may

return to a besetting interest."
"There's apparently a correlation
between objects in

this world and
the objects of people's desires. Whether,
as some hold," a nod

for the painter, "objects
here are created
entirely by will—or,

as I have assumed, things take place
within a range of
what is deserved,

I don't know. But perhaps
no one wanted
the sun enough. Or perhaps—" "'Deserved'."

The General seemed amused. "Maybe no one 'deserved' it."
"People assume
things like the sun," the painter,

surprisingly, spoke. "It
only goes to show
you can't assume anything." Silence

set in. I picked up
overtones.
"You're implying that

Cartesian doubt
actually operates here. I can't be sure
you're real, or—" The General

shook his head. "*Not*
operative. One has been over this
endlessly. I'm

real, hence the discussion
is as insipid
as in the other world. But you'll find,

I think, that everything here
was loved in some way,
or suffered from its lack . . . Yvette

may have been a brood cow—
shrieking, but never with laughter
or orgasm, in any bidonville

my tanks wrecked. One of the forgotten
billions, who agree,
mostly, to forget themselves, and

watch through the wire,
nursing . . . But here,
love is the guiding thread." He

thought. "Listen.
               I was in command
of the perimeter of a landing.

Where is immaterial. I wanted to put
as many men as possible
east, into the mountains,

before the inevitable counterattack. Headquarters
disapproved. They wanted
concentrated defense

of the port, leaving
the hills to the bombers.
They dawdled. I moved

small groups, those highest skilled
at isolated fighting and
ambiguous relations with base,

into the foothills. Too few.
Far too few. I should have been
more cautious. I was inspecting

forward positions. Suddenly
shells exploded
just those few yards off

that let one still be afraid. Trees went down.
I saw
prison camp, years of brooding. There are fads

in war," he scowled, "as everywhere—They might
not be taking prisoners. My jeep was destroyed
under me. My driver

could not walk
and I carried him
the two miles back to base. It took ten hours,

making up for Anchises . . . I wonder if
someday he'll look me up. I was that far
from my pills,

my measured flask. My strategy
was vindicated
I learned, after ten hours

doubting. My
rangers had absorbed
the counterattack, and

now we were moving out.
        And Charles was alive
when we reached base. Barely. But *alive*."

           "It means something
to him," the painter observed. "Heroism.
Manhood." I: "Why not?

Let him be loved
for that. It backs his point
but doesn't answer mine. You, he, Yvette

might all be phantoms," and
I started to say, tormentors: I didn't
remember such emotions. Didn't

say it. Burst out: "I'm here
in borrowed clothes, in a borrowed house,
in a borrowed—" "You are

        genuinely welcome to them—"
said the General,
concerned. But the painter

broke in: "What do you have in mind?"
And they watched me
for that. The chaise, the comfortable armchair

facing my couch . . . I remained
lost in the story; my
shoulders ached for the burden,

my legs for the wound. And then I soared
out of it: "My place
is far from here, far

north," I said. "Beyond the river
and those impassible cliffs.
There are lakes

like those of my childhood, yet purged
of man, of industry. A clean wind,
free of salt, invites the ice.

Where I am
it is always almost winter, the harvest past,
no more effort

possible or needed. My place
is different from this: great
clouds of leather, slung

on thin aluminum rods. And that black
plastic, so tasteful
if handled right. And wood

tortured into knots
by barbarians so savage
the viewer is glad

I made it into art... When I stand
with my hands clasped
behind my back, a transparent

yet intimidating pose, it isn't glass
I look through
at the undying green

of my trees, and their red
and bronze and gold, chasing each other
up hillsides, but a force-field—

I deserve
one of those, I used the word
all my life on faith. Visitors

will come to hear me talk, for hours,
like Hitler or Stalin, yet
not boring at all—so that rule too

will be broken, and no one will want to be free.
I will be
so gracious, each new

martyr, to art,
to science, to liberty, will wish
spontaneously upon arrival here

to make his report—"
                    "What about women?"
the painter

flashed his ugly grin; yet there was
envy in his tone
and well-hidden gaze. "Martyrs to beauty,"

mused the General. Nothing
occurred to me, then, except to
wonder about the Countess. We sat

and drank
in a community of interest
wider than our differences. There was no sun,

no sunset. "Dinner, messieurs,"
                                        trilled Yvette,
back in uniform.

The Countess
presided, wearing
another flaming white

thing, and
one jewel. She seemed,
not distant, unreachable—

as if the wit,
the remarks, and
a certain demand

on my part, for
clarification, merely
halved the distance. The question of solipsism

came up, the range and power
of the imagination. I described
my house again, the leather and aluminum,

meaning no offense
to her taste. "Not at all,"
she smiled, "everyone needs a home.

Mine involves,
I admit, something hotel-like. Strangely enough,
I find that nurturant." She would visit me,

she said. Had never crossed
the river, or seen
the north.

        The painter looked bored.
He and the General
argued

tactics—stupid and
mulish, respectively,
so that the Countess laughed. I

told stories
from my life, played it for laughs,
got laughs. The General

told stories about generals: Vinegar
Joe, Dugout Doug, Black
Jack, emphasizing

their human traits. Crystal
rang, gleamed. Grouse followed turbot;
wine followed wine, including,

she told me, the true Falernian.
The painter described
languidly

the last seventeen martinis
of Dylan Thomas.
                The vines beyond

the dining room windows,
lit by our lights,
moved in the wind. We moved

to the salon. The Countess
suddenly said she would phone
a particularly scintillating group

for another party. We
heard her delighted laughter, far away.
She has never

been oppressed,
I thought (without follow-up,
heavy after dinner). Yvette

sat, prim
by the sideboard, the dishwasher
sighing behind her. The painter

went randomly sullen, the General
wistful: "She should
invite my second wife,"

he said. "Though she wouldn't
fit in. Unless she
dreamed of sophistication

later. Otherwise
she could invite
my dead friends." "Why don't you

ask her?" He only
smiled, and I—
wanting to be at one

with the body
and its company—
regretted asking.

                                       Yvette
came to my room, later, what she wanted
clear in her grin. "Ah, cherie,

charmante portière de cet enfer délicieux,
I am too tired
and too drunk." "Has not Monsieur

discovered," she asked, toying
with my cape, "one needn't be tired?"
                                        And it was true.

We rendezvoused,
the Countess and I,
by the main door. She led me

past the squash courts,
the golf course—grass
untended, a non-golf era

had entered.
                Day rose
gradually. Why

"gradually" was hard to say
without shadows.
      Birds sang

everywhere—
even, I thought,
in the obscure direction.

We walked east in silence,
behind us the windows
opened to the air.

The house lay like a ship.
High above it
a flag caught the wind:

        three legs running
around a common center,
sinister, on a deep burgundy

field. "What sign is that?" I asked.
"The trisceles," she said. "It's a symbol
of various out-of-the-way,

independent places. The Isle of Man
for one. Also
if one follows Jung

on the arrangement of things in threes—" "Ah,"
I said.—"Its motto is
'jetero circumque stabit',

'wherever you throw me I will stand'."
        I liked this,
said so. "But

why is it flying over your
place? Is it your symbol?" "No.
Yours." "Ah,"

I repeated.
"Listen,
shouldn't I be addressing you as

'your ladyship' or something? I mean
you are a—" "Yes, but it doesn't matter.
You may think of me,

but only think, mind,
as Maggie."
                    A path

paved with red stones
amidst the waving grass
seemed the most dreamlike thing. We crossed

fields of daisies
and a tributary
of the distant river. She paused on the other side,

removed her sandals, took
pins from her hair
and shook it free.

I felt
lost in her beauty, and
clumsy. She neither smiled nor frowned,

only took stock
of her thoughts, which, I thought,
were like all this.

                    We came to a meadow
framed by pines,
and low hills, with

a small open structure: white
dome and columns. Under the dome
a kind of lens;

beneath, a simple pallet
bed. She led me
with that firm grasp,

sexier than any hesitation,
up the steps,
unsnapped her robe and lay down,

closing her eyes as if
against the absent sun. I
lay naked beside her

and with fingertips stroked
from shoulder to full
nipples, to belly and side and thigh,

then with full hand
softly, then not as softly, storing
impressions. Till she clutched me

roughly, pulled me to her
with almost a sung, held note. I wasn't sure
when I began to feel

my hand on her breast—
or I could say
mine—

                                        the touch
too rough a moment before,
now too gentle; the furred belly

grazing her side
so casually, its attention elsewhere, that
her thighs wanted

not so much to loosen, as
to speak to it—
            so that I

drew back, frightened, yet
not far, because
I felt her

feel me draw back, and yearn towards me, lips
aching like mine, while
                        my

breasts, cunt, thighs
swelled, filled, softened,
spread . . . and I

spread through his
arms and shoulders and ass, felt
the muscles of his back

flex, wondering why he didn't
clutch that soft thing
beneath him, and spear it, spear it . . . I

entered her. I felt
her feel that, and
                    my sweat beneath her hand, and

my balls, strange from outside,
funny and noble and precious, against
                                    my

thigh ... The face
staring rapt
yet not condemned

in its absorption, while she saw
her own: wild, shy, then
wilder. I see what you mean

by "wetness," I hear what you
like in that sound, do you
like it, oh

please ... Moved, then, towards the core
of her mind, all
concentred now,

rich and various and vital,
while she in me
                    saw

pride, an essential
harmlessness, and
something I couldn't see

which didn't matter. When
our tension
gathered, and

broke, I
understood that, and she
felt me pour

into her; that light
augmented
between our facing mirrors.

                              As we awoke,
separating was
a loss beyond pain.

Lying in my arms, she
spoke: "Now you see
it is possible."

                                        She had scheduled
the party for Friday, but that night,
sans Yvette, we

went for a ride.
              "To the Settlement,"
the General growled. Nothing

further. I wasn't interested. I
wanted to stay home
and think.

                      She gently insisted.
She wore white; I,
her gift, an

ivory and amber
trisceles.
        The General drove

the golf cart. (He wore
the black of action. Of a man
still to be reckoned with.) The painter

bore on his lap
a wicker basket
of the cellar's dustiest finest. In protest

he smoked, tossed
butts onto the darkening
green. Deep in the woods

we parked, followed
the faintest of paths.
This wasn't

the beloved
forest of my awakening.
Trees like Egyptian pillars,

yielding only to
long hard beaks, patient
worms. Low-hanging moss

created a deeper twilight. Dark needles fell.
How had the trees
grown so high

in one another's light?
I stayed close to the others,
lost. Being lost

posed a question: could one merely
wish to be found, or
must one invent

yet another
world to walk
out of the forest to . . . Rush-lights ahead

greened the mist. Something
knocked us to the ground. The Countess shrieked.
The painter swore. I

knelt, drew my sword and
hacked at greasy strands. "Take it easy,"
the General muttered. *They*

surrounded us, silently
urged us
forward. Sheathe your sword,

the General signalled. A ritual,
I thought, rituals must be
few but important here.

We came to a clearing. "Who comes?"
                              "A friend
with friends," said the Countess

firmly. "I know you . . ." The chieftain
advanced into firelight. "And
these." He looked at me. White-haired

like the General, harsh
shadowed features.
Furs, comfortable rags. He

drew the net from us,
turned away. Movement
above: watchers

in the high boughs, with spears,
astonishingly old guns. The hovels
and lean-tos

stank. Ragged
    silent people
merged with the mist. Each wore

some bright spot. Amber.
A patch. They were
    so shy

that I was moved
when they smiled
and brought food—thin

stew, thick
bread. "They're in hiding."
the painter said. "From what,

here?" "From nothing,
'here'," he mocked. "They're
under the Countess' wing.

They don't do much. Make
pots and shit. They'll
sing, presently.

Serbo-Croat,
I think she told me, or some other
fucked-over language. It

drags. One song says
'The day will come', but they don't
remember what it will bring.

They sleep, mostly. You could try
your theory on them—tell 'em they don't exist,
or only in your mind. They might get

a kick out of it.
They might agree." He
                          went in search of more food,

leaving me
among them. "What we see here
is cowardice.

Self-pity. The delight
in stinking." The General
spoke loudly, yet

none of those
clustering round seemed
to heed him, only

what I would say:
                "I didn't think
you liked this." "In the midst

of death," he harrumphed, "I like to believe
I am in life."
"But you aren't," I pointed out. "And these

never were." Now
                  wine, arduously made
from mysterious berries

deep in the woods, passed to me in a chalice.
But the ritual
centered on her: squaws and maidens

brought her weaving; men,
carved animals.   "She puts them

away somewhere," the painter
chuckled, drifting back. "They
clash." More

food came round: river trout, each bite
hallowed, I thought,
eaten in safety.

The chief, in his smoky room,
did not look up
when I entered, yet was

aware of me. Suddenly
I had nothing
to ask him. He had

left the feast
early. It was a matter
of leaving the feast early.

I looked at wall-hangings.
One especially.—Turned
back towards the fire. She

danced—with young braves, grizzled
oldsters; something
primitive, in a ring, with

handholdings. A young girl, hair
braided, came up, motioned me
to join. What vile life

of beatings and pig-sloppings
had she surpassed
for this triumph? I

danced, I seemed to know
the steps. "Where were you from?"
I asked; she put

her hand to her mouth, and fled. Their
songs had an ancient rage: modes too stern
to degenerate into tunes.

Handsome dogs barked, strong
and trusting. The General,
arms folded, avoided

contact. "The other day,
while I was in the Garden
I saw armed horsemen. Are you

aware of them? Are they scouts
of these people?"
    "They are scouts, but

not of this Settlement."
    "Who are they, then?"
"The enemy," he said easily. I

took a deep breath. "We'll talk later,"
he forestalled me,
smiling now. "Wait—" "Her ladyship

does, after all," he said,
"command a strategic pass..."
                    and attended

the Countess, who
joined me, her face
smoke-streaked, her gown sweaty,

and took my hand.
Behind her, the painter
stolidly carried

the gifts—votive offerings
of some unnameable plea. *They
had to sleep*

now, heaped
together between mud walls. The
General led the way

out, stamping, his
back very straight. Guards
watched us go. They were happier

watching and tracking,
I thought, than at anything. On
a shield,

on the medallion
round my neck, the same insignia
caught the dying fire

that I had seen
in the chieftain's hut, and to which,
I knew,

we had no right.
                              "You may have noticed
that at any given time

you won't find
Yvette, her ladyship, myself and
our young friend

together in one room."
                              "Well, Yvette has her
chores ... and the Painter,

I thought he was working somewhere."
                                              "Hardly."
He smiled. "Unfortunately, there is an enemy

and someone must always stand guard.
Oh, we can risk
a few minutes here and there

when there's a party
and Yvette serves. Each of us carries an alarm,
I in my wrist chronometer,

her ladyship,
I believe, in a jewel. Everyone who stays
any length of time receives one."

"Will I - " He
nodded at my medallion. "Who *is* the enemy?"
I demanded. "How can there be

an enemy?" "Well, there just is, you know. This isn't
the Land of Cockaigne,
despite what some might think. And

over the years
her ladyship has sanctioned
an intelligent defensive posture."

He hesitated. "We've all too
little to go on.
Odd sightings.

A broken tree.
A lawn, trampled. Some stock
seized from the dairy farm, a crop despoiled."

"She has a farm?"
       "On the far slope
of the west range. Where did you think

the food came from?" But I was visualizing
some marauder
swooping upon us

in the pavilion, or
on our walk back, and was suddenly mad
with retrospective fear

for her. Why hadn't she told me?
—Dismissed that. Why should she
have to fear anything? I was glad

she hadn't told me. It
wouldn't have been noble. "Couldn't you—
I started to say Think them,

wish them
away—the verb I
could never settle on. "Yes?"

He waited. The salon
                      had never looked better
than on that morning. The vases

gleamed, the paintings
showed cunningly
in that light. Someone was reading

a late *New Yorker*. The current
crop had arrived: *P.M.*, *Vanity Fair*,
transition, still

going strong somewhere. It was a room
that could outface eternity.
Always the new

work would come in, the most recent music and people.
I squared my shoulders.
"Show me what I must do."

                                        He led me
through the kitchen, past brooms and tools
and a steel double door; down

many steel steps to an elevator
that opened at a word, and
descended so long

he had to pee when we reached
the corridor. Flashing
lights. Wires. A place

anyone from our world
would recognize as central.
It was exciting,

and ridiculous (I told myself).
Our footsteps echoed. Yvette
was in the command post,

smoking,
nervelessly watching the board,
her right hand

cuing the monitors: the farm.
The golf course. The house,
three views. The pavilion.

The near slopes. The Garden.
With her left hand
she tapped out her report:

/nothing/. I
noticed the hiss of air, the irreducible
buzz

beneath subdued muzak. "You are relieved
early, my dear." The General
cleared his throat. "I

shall train our friend." "D'accord,"
she said, and left, weary and
serious. For three hours

he initiated me, hovering
beside the swivel chair. The
board. The console.

Simulated drills. My own
fire and radiation gear.
"If we 'wished' them away," he said,

"they would damn well 'wish' themselves back.
Some things can't be avoided.
And understand this: if

we must fight here—and I pray
we needn't—
we are fighting for our home."

The medallion
emitted a clear note. He
stared at the board, screamed: "Get on it!

This one's real!" "I'm not prepared,"
I screamed, but he was
pounding down the corridor: "I must

see to her ladyship—" I swung
to the board. Attack
in force: tanks, planes, heavy guns;

as he had predicted, right through
the pass, their goal
the river. How had they

sneaked into position? The TV monitors
were burnt out in the first
minute. I relied

on pluridimensional grids generated
by too many sensors to destroy.
Above, our

missiles rose, robot fortresses
threw off their cover. I analyzed
vectors, remembered

more than he had taught me—
perhaps from another life,
or somehow from my own. The enemy

stumbled into our
traps, our emplacements.
Between waves I smoked. Yvette

had left her cigarettes. An image of
her and the Countess,
raped, wrenched me. I could fight

to be worthy of them, though no worth
had been asked. I could fight
for the paintings and flowers. I was fighting

for my self, which death itself
had not been able to destroy.
Explosions

rocked my vents, dimmed my lights. I smashed and
smashed on the console.
                                      After some time

the board was clear, except for
Damage signs.
The elevator worked,

strange without his presence. The seal
held on the double door, the wheel turned.
I pushed against rubble.

                                        Light
too far inside. The roof gone.
The fridge

lay on its side, its fruits scattered.
Blackened
beams fell. I improvised

surfaces to stand on.
—The grey cat, still. In the house,
no other bodies.

                They lay on the lawn
on the parterre, by
the oddly untouched pool,

among robots: shining forms,
fallen, or frozen in triumph. The board had misled me
I saw no artillery

or planes—only their knives,
Saturday Night Specials,
clawed hands.

                Who was that faded burgher,
almost untouched
down to the absent half? I invented

a fate for him, a retribution:
a grammar-school bully, that fact
buried beneath the failed

stocks, the well-meant marriage.
Had he even
been armed?—People I'd overheard

making stupid remarks
at modern art museums.
Muggers, or

would-be muggers, near
rapists of
friends . . . Kids. Several

hippies—headbands, beads around
gore. Terrifying to
see them again . . . did you discover

the Infinite Unity
here, scum? A probable
boss, broken, once

hated sight
unseen in his inner office. Some
forgotten coffeehouse

face, still
opinionated
above its shattered chest, some Est crut

who had said
we choose everything . . . Obvious
subway talkers. But

who was that ugly mother
and child? Had the kid
cried, in some stinking

bus? I
held her, shook her,
                    asking.

They came apart.
There must be
genuinely evil people. Not

enough. I hadn't
planned this.
Had never forgiven them.

I would have. I would have.
I hadn't.—What had they
wanted? To swim,

to nourish their squalling brats
by poolside,
to find the river.

                My four friends
weren't among them. Perhaps in fragments . . . or
had reached the forest. Perhaps they would

reformulate themselves
and this place, for another
guest. Even

these might rise again, as in
Isaiah, or *Night of the Living Dead*.
I foresaw

an infinite regress
of such scenes, a pursuit. But
that couldn't be true,

I'd thought of it . . .
                      I arose,
shook this off, still

talking without stop
to them. I
missed her already

but would not search. Would
wash off this blood
in the river, and head downstream.

Fire spread, crackling, among
the ruins I had held. Smoke
sullied the empty sky.

I took off my cape
and laid it over the mother, and flung the trisceles
among them . . . pleased with the gesture.

Juggernaut was grazing
the edge of the burnt area,
gazing toward the palace.

I
hailed him, mounted,
thinking he looked marginally

more like a horse.

2

It was dark when I reached the town.
For miles

we had passed
thatched-roofed villages
                              barely breaking the horizontal,

carrot, potato fields, tiny
orchards
scratched into the common.

Few lights showed. Few forms
stood in the doorways, smoking long pipes—
nodding, or staring at my animal.

I left him
where grass came up to a wall. He
turned without sentiment

toward where the river, now wide and calm
somewhere to the north,
divided meadows.

A mud-rut street.
                     Lamps, their fuel obscure.
A tavern sign . . . dim

yellow light, not inviting. I
entered.
Men, a barmaid

looked, fell silent.
                  Beer,
I grunted; luckily the word was the same.

I paid, I
seemed to have the coin—some brutal head.
                                What was I

in these eyes, slowly turning away? Freebooter,
hired knife, following my own orders
for someone else's pay . . . it was appealing, and

doubtless a useful role
here: hadn't I seen
the dead live

and die and live again? But
                        I didn't want that . . .
They saw a predator.

God knows what they had been
to like that lumpy soup,
this beer, their rags. Whether they

had land to work, or
a place in an early factory,
or had died for land to work,

no priest's, no duke's man
would come for grain or gold,
in a bad year, with the wife sick

and the soldiers gone with the boy . . . Maybe,
once in a century, a
rough, pointless joke, deeply

savored. I didn't know.
I only bowed
my head, wanting

only not to be
one of the strong,
the lucky ones. I would sit

forever over this beer. Slowly
the body would ooze away;
contempt breed familiarity.

                              At length,
one of them, foul-
breathed, handed me

a slip of paper.
                "You go—here."
A number, an unreadable name. Outside,

I followed blue numbers
on white tin squares downhill.
The lamps were

gas, possibly, that one step
up
already a risk... A confused flight

of peasants and animals passed.
                              What was "death," here?
Merely a sleep, more dawns... Perhaps

this watchfulness
itself was hell. No.
I wasn't tired. I was glad

to leave that tavern. Would not be made
a scapegoat. They'd made a mistake
in letting me go.

I was strong now. I would use
this summons, whatever it meant.
A City lay ahead.

String quartets
came from there, and noble people.
                                            The number. I

climbed dark stairs. A door
opened, far above. No eyes
watched from the cracks.

One can be
trapped on a staircase . . .
                                   She had opened

the door, then sat
again at the table
in the bare room.

                       "Susan," I said.
Yet it was not she
because her smile

was eager, though her eyes
had the remembered vagueness.
And she was beautiful: would not take care

here more than before
for her dress, but it would
always be right; a few automatic gestures

would be enough to smooth
the brown hair with its buried tints.
The long white fingers

were free of nicotine-stains,
the brow never drawn or lined. "They
said you were here," she said. "I mean

that someone had come
like the man I'd described."
                              "You were a suicide,"

I said stupidly. "So were you,"
—gently, not quarreling.
                              "Why you, I wonder?"

I murmured. It seemed
trivial it should be she,
at a level where

anyone would be trivial. "Oh . . . it was the only thing.
I'd left home
too often before to forgive

their taking me back from
that hospital. Parents are such fools, always,
aren't they? Especially when they're wise.

You said that once. And after
what Jack did to me, I was too tired
to patch together some

farce of emotions and call it
me. It was the
third or fourth time I'd tried it,

I wasn't being hysterical." "No—I
didn't mean why you
died, but

why you're the one to
appear. I haven't met
anyone I knew

personally."
                She smiled. "Would you like some tea?"
I was startled. "Tea would be delightful." And

there was a stove
in the shadows, a sink, tea things.
Place mats

for the scarred table. She hummed
while she worked, fragments I remembered; lit
a candle, and

within me, another
dubious surprising light. "You despised me,"
I said. She: "I didn't 'despise' you.

I always respected your mind.
But you were so . . . "
" 'Importunate'," I said. She nodded, that

sage, stalling gesture I remembered.
"It was as if you
couldn't . . . relate to anyone except

physically, and I wasn't
very attracted to you." (I liked that "very".)
"And at that point I was

committed to the marriage—" She paused.
We laughed. The words were absurd.
"But I've had time, here—"

"Five years. Between the time
you died and I—"
I stopped. "And I found

I was thinking about you a lot . . .
I missed your viewpoint."
                    I stirred my tea, watching

the shadow of my spoon
in candelight. The room
smelled of wood and tea

and milk and
the lemon she had cut.
Beyond the narrow windows

two drunks
laughed, sought
ever-receding clarifications, sang

in some awkward, homey
early-teutonic gangue. A thousand years
would not be enough to relax in

after their lives. I imagined
another life: one of
the billion apartments; a wife

with her problems, I with mine,
sitting at morning or evening; children
bringing us their problems, language

always returning to Start . . .
Watching them. Striking without embarrassment
the necessary poses. Now

for a moment
it was all possible again. We were alive
after some happy ending.

Had just moved in
and could talk
wallpaper, subscriptions, the second car

with that note
of bright, self-astonished improvisation.
And I would have a job

I identified with, and she the strong
hope for one—so that
my endless reassurances

could cease. My boss
would be my friend, his
problems taken to heart, his wife

her friend—
          And then she looked at me, one
bleak, perhaps remembering

glance amidst that sweetness,
and we were
what we had always been: intellectuals discussing the cave

we might share awhile, one eye out
for pursuers.
          "Is this your

'heavenly mansion'?" I asked, hating the
language one brought
with one, the engrained

sneer. "Oh no," she said,
looking off. "That is very far away.
It always was. I never expected

to go there immediately." "Neither did I.
There's time,"—trying to catch,
then avoiding her eye, knowing

that whatever developed
now, there would be
no room for me

in her place, or her in my
cold northern realm. I asked
what she had done with her time.

Read, mostly. Once in a while
she went into town. The Library was
as grey and noble

as it should be, with a park
and plaza where poets spoke
to crowds as if conversing. "Some famous names,

some unknown but very good." Even
the rarest materials
could be borrowed. I noticed

on a small shelf
the golden clasps
of thick brown folios. A complete

Sophocles. Aristotle's dialogues.
The Q Document. And the radio, she said,
played the lost music—

Schubert's lost Seventh,
a lovely, lilting
tomorrow-to-fresh-fields sort of tune

from the scherzo was
a local theme song.
The Bach cantatas

people had wrapped fish in.
Now I tried
to rid my face of mistrustfulness

and let
the hungry man
inside, show. "Did you

stay in touch with Jack?" she asked,
"I haven't called him." "I rarely saw him,"
I said. "You know,

Ruth left me." She seemed startled
that I had mentioned it; I realized
she had assumed

Ruth had left me. I
smiled. "Funny how one always asks." "Yes, isn't it!
As if I cared, really . . ." The round face

blushed, and I knew
what else she had been doing:
taking her time

at last, over men, over
fantasies, and I wondered
what strange lovers

had come up those stairs, not
having to wait,
lost and brooding at the tavern. "Jack was

an ordinary little man." I said. "I would
see him around town . . .
And that woman he found

was ordinary too. Little
attentions, little devotions—he had that
slightly hysterical look

educated American males of
my generation had
when they found someone. Yet I think

that every day
he found himself listening
to the void you left, where she put only

something rather squeaky. Not
having to be told
she was beautiful, not being beautiful,

or to be held
endlessly, being told
her horrible past was not there. I don't know

how he described his feelings.
He probably said
he was happy. He was superficial."—Two

tears appeared, dropped. I had
exacted them because
she hadn't always loved me.

The teacup trembled unregarded.
The room seemed warm.
Slowly she touched my face. "It's all lies,"

I growled. "You're simply another
demon. You couldn't love me."
                              "Can't you accept it?"

she asked softly
and set the teacup down
and stood, like a woman, waiting,

by which I knew
she was utterly changed
and real.

           And so we went to bed. I had a vision
of the calendar—so many days
since my first love for her, now

fulfilled,
minor events intervening. I gloried
in the little hairs

around her nipples, and in protesting
that they were sexy. "I guess I didn't
wish them away enough." And in

her response: shyness
giving way to lean
frenzy. (The thought

of the Countess' machine
flicked by; I
ignored it.)

The leaded windows
fogged with our heat. During the night
we awoke. There was something naughty

in stealing time from sleep. At one point
that rude speech
boiled from the tavern, distant and

harmless—a Breughel, no sombre Greuze.
At dawn
we made plans (reheating

the tea, wiping
a space in the window
staring at the fog). I would go

to the City. Had imagined
arriving there alone, but asked
"Will you go with me?"

"Not yet,"
—with that dear,
too-conscious delicacy. "I have some matters

to wind up here." "But you will come?"
"Yes. Find us a place
and I'll join you."

"You'll trust me."
"Of course. We can always change." She had
no phone (had hated phones); I was to call

the Pear Tree.
                        Now that I had
a task to perform in the City

I felt its master. Yet over breakfast
I worried about
transportation. Regretted

Juggernaut, though
objections to him remained. I
described him to her, but

she didn't recognize
what I described, and it seemed
distasteful to her. And I needn't worry

how to reach the City:
there were rent-a-cars,
trains, buses ... any number of ways.

                                        I caught the first bus.
Rickety, serviceable; only
a number, on a smudged

card in the windshield. But I thought
they all must go to the City.
                          Boarding

I did not pay
the swarthy, silent driver. While waiting
I had decided

the service was nationalized.
                              Hills and valleys,
teased by shifting fog. The river

and other rivers flowed
under bridges, past willows and cypresses.
Barges passed, heavy with goods.

                      A madman
papered with tiny stickers
got on at the next stop, some

empty cornfield crossroads; ignored
the driver's barking laugh, sat
towards the front, not looking at me.

He had wandered,
I thought, perhaps from roads like these—one more terror
of onrushing headlamps, mere

pain could not change him.
                         Here,
tavernkeepers would

insult but feed him. He would learn
to joke and grin for a drink; eventually,
out of boredom, perhaps, invent

coherence.
                  Market women
got on. I was astonished

that they were still—
or again—old, or
if young, wore

                    that black,
or those cheap prints
(the first created need

which had filled
both worlds, apparently) and were carefully
blind to me. They

greeted each other with smiles, hugs,
clumsy words.
                    We passed both

rustic places like Susan's—heavy
eaves, moss-grown walls—
                    and filling stations,

twenty-four-hour markets
where sports cars stopped and big
motorcycles.
                         A gang stood drinking.
They looked happy; some old song
of endless road ahead

had come true. Tonight they would enter
one of the villages.
              A Mercedes

dogged the bus, played, passed us.
(I berated myself
for taking the first pokey bus.) I considered

the minimal difference
between worlds on
this stretch, at least, of the road. Was one satisfied

with so little: a Harley, flourishing turnips? But
I wouldn't be satisfied,
I thought, and

relaxed on the springless seat. Someone I
could talk to—another
painter, it turned out—staggered on

at some real or imitation-
Tudor tavern.
A mob of timeless cronies cheered him off.

Short, moon-faced. "A new boy!"
he laughed, in rich Australian.
                    "How does one tell?"

He shrugged. "Where you headed?"
"I thought there was
only one place."

"—That's 'ow we tell. Yer on yer toes
still. There's lots of places. But,
'ell, go to the City

if you must."
"Where else is there?"
He gazed, grinning, out; described

what had happened
when the London galleries
decided the colonial thing

was played out. *He* hadn't changed—
or his abbos, sitting and drinking
in submarine sort of places, far away,

the one perfected image. Suddenly one had no friends,
and a choice: to do
the mature thing, fly home

to carve one's cracked block of soap, or go
into mourning in Earl's Court. "Well you know
which I chose." His continual

chuckles, shrugs,
and everything he said
were mannerisms,

the eyes were an ancient statue's,
the paint rinsed away. "I needed"
he summed up, "more love

than was available, and I died
like Kit Marlowe,
stabbed through the eyeball in a pub." Cool, I

asked if he'd ever heard
here, of
my painter, described his work. "Nope. Sorry."

Realism, "retrospective"
realism was the last
rage he had noticed. He had met

big names: Picasso
was at work,
I'd be glad to hear. "Wow," I said; I had

forgotten Picasso. "What sort of stuff?"
"As per usual. What else?
He's run through

five or six girls since he arrived.
They're more agonized types
now, and he listens more

but the work is the same. What's missing?"
he demanded, gesturing through the rattling
window at the fog,

lifting now. "The sun,"
I said gloomily, still
wondering if I should feel

gloomy about it. "Good!
                              Shows yer on yer toes!
(Bloody idiot.) I meant in the

dorfs. The little villages." I
looked a long time,
suggested various things. Life. Hope.

He wouldn't help me.
"Churches," I realized,
                         observing the market women

with new respect. "Now if you want
a *significant* encounter," he said,
"get off at the third stop after this,"

and got off
at a place indistinguishable
to my eyes, from his last; but I suppose

the beer was better
and the company. The third stop lay
downhill from a large building,

its front a light windowless stone. Rising
tiers of small, rounded arches.
I didn't recognize it

and as I climbed
the smooth lawn, I thought I
seemed to have entered

(when?) the territory
of other people. The wall
carried no legend. Few surfaces

bore writing here.
                      The door creaked.
Within: cold light,

folding chairs,
a big wooden cross. It was too big,
and the room was too big. Only around the walls,

under the windows, some softness:
lilies. A tray
of glasses filled

with red, dusty wine,
set out as if for a wedding.
To the side, a small room

with a cot, a laden
crucifix, the remains
of a herring dinner. He

was tending flowers, or polishing
something already clean; the hunched back
in its long brown coat was

turned to me. "Do you . . .
work here?" The drawn face,
                              the astonishing eyes

watched me a moment,
turned. "You're alone,"
I tried.—Slight accent:

"I have you." Knowing
suddenly who he was, I marveled
that he had learned English. But

there had been time, and,
certainly, other
intruders. The room, though large,

smelled musty. The long hands,
cutting, cherishing,
fascinated me. Had he ever

touched her?
Or anyone? There had been
those whores in Berlin, after Schelling's lectures;

or were they
also a story,
part of the plot

to put her off?
                I stared at the cross.
So large, so carefully bare

it suggested nothing. A plus sign.
Kierkegaard
came up beside me

and stood with folded hands. Would he offer me
wine, I wondered. "You expected to

find him," I murmured. "Yes. You not?" "I . . . was Jewish,"
I said awkwardly.

He shrugged, a painful
surge in that twisted frame,
and I remembered

what he had said: that any attempt
to resolve the contradictions
of this life within this life

was Judaism . . . But this
was no longer that life, and I
regarded him—conscious

of the strong, foursquare body
I had wished for myself—
with vague contempt.

                        Then felt bound
to explain the position
I had held, and in

that bright-student's tone
I hated, emitted
a string of abstractions,

feeling dreadfully American. He
listened, looking at nothing.
"Where do you think we are?" he asked.

"I don't know.
I was thinking I'd
find a scientist. He could explain

the principle. And maybe
they've worked out
a way back—" I stopped. My words had run on

without me. He showed
the first faint interest.
"Where do *you* think we are?"

"We are in hell," he said.
                              "I could adduce
against that," I

attempted a laugh, "the arguments of Belial:
we eat well, we have this
imaginative power

you haven't, for some reason,
availed yourself of—"
I restrained myself. He was

gazing at the cross. "Why didn't you
look him up, then? Or did you?" "One doesn't
'look him up',"

Kierkegaard snapped. "He looks you up,
and is always looking.
He harrowed hell

once, and may again. I hope for this.
It is my hope. And to meet him
is not to meet

as men do, as you and I
do. Questions, correctly formulated
for the first time, will become

their own answers in his presence.
He does not clasp one's hand
as you might mine. Simply, he will be there

and take me to his bosom . . .
                             The man I might meet
in some low alley

here, tending the sick—should any
consent to be sick—is just a man;
                             or less,"

he added; the implied
doubt of my
metaphysical status seemed

not worth my while to dispute. "Why
'hell', though . . . ?"
He smiled oddly.

                   "Hell is argument."
"Well, why are you here?
You didn't deserve it . . . by your lights, you had

'faith', etc." "Please don't be base," he said.
"I have been here a long time.
Please don't be utterly base."

He moved away again.—I said,
"I suppose where you went wrong
was to think that a mere physical breakdown,

even a physical stoppage, would prove anything. It's
consciousness itself
that has to be played out

in all its horrible permutations. I've been wondering
if it starts
before we do—but that's irrelevant. In fact, the whole

concept of a start,
or an end, is wishful thinking.
I guess what you're doing here

is refining your personality,
year after year in this room,
into an essence, an agony that

won't be a thought any more . . . I must sit down,"
I said, and sat.
Memories, carefully avoided,

had come. He sat beside me,
his hands on his knees.
                    "You can tell me."

And for the first time
I spoke
of irremediable things. I don't know

how much he understood: night flights, weeping
on machines across continents,
as if it had been my choice

to stage my petty drama
as a spectacle. I also mentioned
wars, mass murders,

revolutions—those that came
and those that didn't; meanwhile curious
why he had asked. Perhaps

listening was
a penance—
no understanding required. When I stopped,

he spoke: "Are you quite sure
God means nothing?"
                        "I had an idea

of a presence, but its point
was its silence. Now
I'm silent too," I said, running on again.

                        "You might still try..."
"'Chastity'?" I snarled.
                        "Or thinking of

Another
more than yourself." "I try,
I do try

sometimes," I sighed, disregarding
the capital letter.
I rose. I had hoped

for dialectic, for his irony
to blow me away. It had been
our great joy. But he felt,

probably, that had been life
and life was done; had put off
the masks with revulsion.

At the door I looked back. He was
smiling at his hands. "You should
not have sought me out,"

he said. "You should have sought out something
strong and confident and growing."
—I mumbled something, stepped

into the lukewarm afternoon. Wondered
if invisible quotation marks
had surrounded the words; if I had

wasted my time
garnering a deep insult. Decided
not to worry. I hadn't

known he was there.
He was an accident.
I hadn't sought him out.

                                         I took a car
from a shopping center lot.
Others were doing it.

Still others
admired, from between
mannequins in windows, or from

little enameled benches, the continual
arrival and departure
of vehicles. I hesitated

between a Maserati, and,
for the privacy, a Rolls,
then grabbed a Triumph. The empty land

gave way to parks,
golf-courses, elm-lined
streets, riding stables. Driving was

especially notional: the car
ran out of gas when I
wanted to stop. Clean restrooms. I, too,

played tag with buses, once hit
200k. Towards four
I saw before me

a government building.
Parked, checked out
rhe other cars. Above the door,

no eagle but a dove. Inside:
offices were clearly marked,
lines moved fast, the people

were nice. Young, mostly, in
shirtsleeves and peasant blouses; what bald heads
and specs I saw were there

for wisdom and byplay. Good
coffee steamed in a corner.
They offered me some.

Asked where I was from. Gave me
a map of the City.
It was big. Loaded me

with guidebooks. I
asked about a place
for me and Susan. They checked the computer,

x'd the map. We'd be on "Neat Street." I
smiled, but
that was the semi-official nickname.

"Nice neighborhood." Also below my name
on the green screen I saw
reference to my north-woods place. I belonged

to various clubs. (Clubs?—Set my face
in sophisticated, British lines.) The Cenacle des Beaux-Arts.
The Rilke-Kreis. And

the Suicides' Club . . . seeing
my distress, they reassured me:
words I heard

were "select." "Elegant." "Recherché." One man
had had lunch there, described
the fireplace, the reading room,

Kurt Gerstein's portrait.
       A girl said, "worthwhile."
They delighted in

service, in
honing the client
to a point

of eagerness, which they shared. Only
when that joy
entered their eyes, a look of steel

entered also, and I thought
of the picket lines
where they had died, the mines and factories;

coughing their lungs out in the dust.
I asked about Kierkegaard. "We've tried
to reach him,"

a boy said. "There's a group
working on it full time." An older man
shook his head: "You can't

do anything with such people."

                                        I entered the City
by roundabout ways,

as did the river. West
of the suburbs one came upon
lakes, marshlands,

a tideless inland port
of interlocking marinas. People
lived by night here.

By day
bartenders polished glasses.
                                      Birds

roosted, fed. Flights
continually rose and settled.
                                      Deer grazed the banks.

It was the will
of the people here, that these animals,
so near the City, should not be hurt.

They had few other
self-appointed tasks. Houseboats
drifted up, docked, were

extended, repainted,
destroyed in
month-long parties or

vanished one morning.
They were painted
with flowers, polka-dots,

harmless violent slogans boasting
godlike feats of
drinking, wenching or the sheer

volume of bullshit
so-and-so, within, was
capable of. There were

                          stabler places; big
condo blocks with
doors that never closed

on people who never slept, but kept
poker games, and
gossip, recipes, horoscopes, wives

flowing from one
balcony to the next,
defying gravity. A

belt of this,
the Zone,
surrounded the City. I

                                  stayed with them awhile
parked, drank; drove on,
then stopped longer. One could

experiment here—
a fistfight
one could win, a three-day drunk

without cost.
                I had decided
to let Susan lie,

temporarily. We would spend
eternity together;
if not, I faced

the pain of breakup
at some future point.
I wanted to demonstrate

not freedom so much as
acausality: that I could
recall her at any time

without guilt.
Meanwhile 1 had one arm
around some blonde: fashion-

model cadaverous, the first
of the two types here. The other,
across the table, was zaftig

and giggled. My date was
primo. Former
art-history major, died some brutal way . . . her frequent

silences, during which she
wanted me to beg
for her thoughts, were

brooding, not just sullen. With my free hand
I gestured, holding
forth to some jerk. They could be very good

on their main thing,
Final Illness. It became
a polished aria, meant to suggest

waste, pathos; was
received in silence,
judged by shifting standards. What had come earlier

was less "worked"; stale
jokes, the superiority
of various towns, races, football teams.

Some had been, they said, rich,
some still struggling, but they
met on the squash courts,

ogled each other's fortunes,
payrolls met, mergers worth billions . . . About
the nature of our eternity

they spoke little, simply thanked god;
resented
my bringing it up. In

the City they liked
mainly shows, dance places and
the punishment cells.—I

                             talked
only during
the second part of my stay

(first I had been
silent, darkly attractive). I was
mocking, as I recall

that night, the continued
popularity of astrology. She'd make me
pay for it later. "Asshole."

"Intellectual snob."—the phrases
lashing from some mumble. Shortly
she'd realize I

was a snob, and I'd go.
I had a speech planned. (And whereas with
Susan, I had

almost forgotten
the Countess' machine, here I was
glad

no one mentioned it.)
                            We were all
drinking, washing down

quaaludes. The topic drifted.
"I sort of
miss my wife and kids," said the

ex-ski instructor
(the one
with the chubby one). "It's sort of a shame

I can't see them. Of course I
don't *want* to see them
too soon . . . I just wish I

could tell them
not to be afraid
of anything." My date wanted

to leave, then. Our boat
rocked amid reeds. Reflections
from the water

moved on the ceiling. Warm, perfumed,
she lay on my arm,
aggrieved even in sleep,

though sometimes she
clung to me
with a murmur,

hard to interpret and
unremembered later. I lay there smoking,
thinking I had to plan. I knew

nothing of science, yet had
always relied on it. I had an address,
and the map the

"angels" had given me (thus I had learned
they were called, and called themselves,
with humor or rue). Was spurred further

by the total
incuriosity of the Zone.
                              We set out

early, she
icy (had wanted
some semi-finals or other). The landscape

was now completely flat.
The usual ground-mist
made it a Campagna,

a Luneberg Heath, someplace
old beyond rejuvenation, yet still
useable. Then the mist lifted

and I saw
the first
towers of the City, the nearer

towers of the Institute. That
rhythm of
arcades, domes and radar dishes, fountains, benches

full of animated people . . . I'd no idea
how vast it was. Possibly it entered
its own strange space, to find

the space it needed.
The day lightened. The parking lot
was immense. She

refused to leave the car,
crossed her arms, glared. I
argued, then realized

I didn't have to.
                    Here was no pompous facade;
anyone might enter

anywhere. I
strode busy corridors. People
smiled at me

over their instruments. I found
Information. Doctor
Renshawe (thus

the name tag; the desk
was functional and anonymous) clasped my hand
with both of his. He wore tweeds

under the open labcoat, smoked a pipe, had
bright, kind eyes. The little office
blazed—was, I thought,

the inverse of a confessional. "I'll probably
ask the wrong questions. Or questions
inherently unanswerable." "The way you describe your error

indicates to me
you won't commit it." "I just
don't want to waste your time." He laughed.

"We seem to have *time*.
And the resources
for personal attention. What's on your mind?"

                                                        "Results.
Where are we?" "Well,
there's some evidence

that the overall shape of space
here is Lobachevskian rather than Riemannian.
Do you—"

I grinned. "Saddle-shaped." "Or, as I
usually have to say
at this point, 'the hand that holds the baseball'.

The values of things,
one G, lightspeed, keep changing, but changing
along a certain curve. Lobachevsky space

might account for this." "So we are literally
'on the other side'?"
"I'm not saying that. Only that space here

is abstractly complementary
to another space."
                        I considered this.

"Why is there no sun?"
                        "Well, that, of course . . .
a 'why' question . . . There's evidence

of a barrier
fifteen to twenty miles up, and solid."
I was horrified. "The underside,"

I said. "The surface of the earth." "Let's not jump
to conclusions. It may not be
earth. Or there may

be no other side.
We have plans,
if we can get the materials, to send up something."

"A rocket." "Well, yes. A small one.
Even if it just
explodes on impact—" "Spectrum reading." He

nodded, fussed with his pipe. "The sky is blue—
by the way—for the usual reasons.
We've no idea

where the heat goes. That also
seems to obey different laws."
"How do you get

materiel?"
         He hesitated. The dry smile
surprised me. "One goes through channels."

         "And at the channels' end?"
"There is a room
where matter is created out of nothing,

apparently in response to need. Or I should say
'things' appear. In physical terms, it's
awkward to speak of 'matter', here."

"Where is this room?" "Downstairs,
by the freight elevators."
"Can I see it?"

"Certainly." "—I was just curious." "It's
a most unspectacular process. And
selective. Our various departments

need,
regularly, things like agar,
pipettes, rare earths, but it's difficult to need

a vane servomotor, if you
see what I mean." "I see what you mean," I said. "It's at
a higher level of abstraction." He

warmed to my sympathy: "If we could
hook *up* something
to it, and actually make *requests*—

but in the meantime
it takes a while." "Couldn't you
sort of sit around

needing? Have teams?"
                                    "We tried that.
And now there are

signs in the rec room
and all the corridors: 'Wishing Don't Make It So.'
There's an unfortunate tendency

to refer to it in the feminine.
I personally
see no mystery about the process, if one

accepts steady-state. Which may
also apply here.
If a single atom

can be 'created', why not that concatenation called
an ehrlenmeyer flask? Perhaps that steel room
is the mouth of a white hole. Perhaps we all are.

That's where things stand."
                              A side door opened;
a girl dropped

a folder on his desk. Renshawe
beamed at her; she at him,
left. "I suppose this

Institute
has always been here."
                    "We like to think so, but our

history is spotty. Perhaps you could
help us with it? You were a
literary type," glancing at the folder. "As I say,

we like to break down barriers." "That's
nice of you, Doctor, but
I've other plans, and

commitments in the City." "Such as?
I'm curious. Strictly personal, I won't
betray you to the thought police."

We both laughed. "I'm not worried,"
I said, "one can
flick danger away,

no doubt you've noticed. If there are
thought police, I'm sure they're
reduced to harmless enthusiasts.—I'll be

setting up housekeeping
with a woman, an old friend. And then,
'hopes of high converse with the mighty dead'?"

He looked
blank at this. "You seem to be
evading the main issue," I said.

He shrugged. "The way
reality apparently 'follows'
the imagination." "No.

                        The fact of death,"
I said with quiet melodrama.
                              "Same answer to that

as to the other: we're physical scientists.
As I see it, if I'm conscious,
if I *remember*, I'm alive. There are places downtown

that pursue the 'spiritual' side of things, and are
well-attended." "But the ultimate goal,
Doctor. The point of your researches.

A way back?"
            He wasn't surprised. "It's too early
to think of that. Far too early . . . I see we belong

to one of the same clubs."
                      "Which?" He
busily filled his pipe. "Oh.

Any others?"
"I'd have to check. You know,
                    I was a failure."

I waited, but
he said no more. Possibly
he too was waiting.

As I opened the door, he placed
my folder in Out. "These come
out of there, too," he murmured,

". . . sometimes she works fast."
                                      In the parking lot
the girl and the Triumph

were gone. In what seemed
an unreasonable provocation, I had to search ten minutes,
found only

a '73 Camaro leaking oil. This was
                                      full City now,
cobblestones,

pizza parlors, hairdressers,
head shops, pet shops, garages.
The sky had darkened,

the lights
gleamed on damp. Too few
movie theatres had that

espresso-in-the-lobby look and
arty titles. The people
above the shops had gone down

earlier, I thought, in
couples, in families,
to take what they needed with

no payment but a smile—
                                 prolonged with more ease
than any smile in life;

and sat now
in television-glow, in those apartments—
the plaster smooth, the plumbing always fast

and sweet, the children calling. I had
imagined it, perhaps; was even
enjoying,

somewhat desperately,
driving through it, negotiating
lane changes

with quaint old trams. Rain fell, my wipers squeaked.
I headed towards
a new hotel complex rising

above all this. And by the time
I had parked, deep underground, and
had gone up

to my suite, I was
tearing at my arms. She would not answer.
Would no longer

be in that room
which carried now
the charm of heaven. She would not want to see me. "Fool!

Pig!" I
raged at myself. The man
at the Pear Tree was *dense*. I shrieked

her name, my name,
waited. Pulled
the drapes shut

on the lights of the City. To stop her thinking
I might have preferred them
to her for one minute.

                    Then she was there,
with calm, marital warmth, saying not a word
about the days and weeks.

"Tomorrow I'll find our place
and take possession. Will you come?"
                                  "Yes, of course."

"I'm sorry I was so long." "It's quite all right—
the City can be quite seductive."
"I've only just

                arrived in the City,"
I said, cursing my honesty. She sounded amused:
"The environs are even more so."

"I miss you."
"Oh, I miss you . . . describe where you are."
I laughed, almost hysterically. "Oh, it's

the classiest hotel room . . . there's a deep tub,
thick grey carpet, a real desk,
the usual headboard tensor lamp, a

firm double bed—" "Mmm."
"Mmmmmm. And probably even—
yes—a Gideon Bible, I'll

take it to bed,
do some more research." "Sleep well.
I'll be there soon." "How *long*?"

"Not long."

Our house,
vine-smothered,

in dark brown brick,
stood at the end of a lane
off Neat Street. One wall was

part of a City wall—still whole, there,
vine- and weed-grown.
                                Lovers at evening

walked on the parapet,
admiring the
trees that grew from it,

the water trickling
from gargoyle heads. There were many Walls
within the City, wide

parks and meadows
between them. A mystery
I pondered, those early days, was that

they seemed to mark a shrinkage, not a growth;
the inner ones were newer. An Esplanade
with a rococo iron fence formed

the inmost ring, around downtown and
the harbor. Houses
buttressed by a Wall

were sought-after. Some Walls were
honeycombed with quaint apartments.
                                        Our house

came alive at twilight. Filtering through the
vines, the Queen Anne windows, it
gilded the

art-nouveau sideboards, counters, mantelpiece.
But the breakfast nook
and private quarters upstairs were filled

with light all day.
Someone had stacked logs
for the fireplace, someone had vacuumed.

                                        In the shops
and boutiques along Neat Street I found
a bed for our room,

hard-edged
plastics and high-tech
for my rooms. Had them hold

couches, armchairs, kitchenware,
pending Susan's approval. I liked
the joy of these craftsmen,

talked colors and textures,
even described
that feeling of marriage, of

household—it was like
being bread, something as
necessary and loved, and was

the only payment they required.
                                        Besides nest-building, I
explored. Had felt

uneasy about the continual
European motif, but
the grid of downtown

reassured me;
               and the skyscrapers:
the Mies thing

from '23, with the glass curves,
a Frank Lloyd Wright needle,
a Mendelsohn breaking wave,

rising among
little gleaming structures.
                             To the southwest,

a Sant'Elia complex, with traffic ramps,
walkways, 100 stories tall. And someone's
Palace of the Soviets. I

noted, early on,
                    the Palace of Justice;
left it for later.

The river,
broad and stately,
entered its estuary. I crossed

airy footbridges
twelves times a day, carrying packages,
moving with cheerful crowds, passing

other cheerful crowds. The water was clean,
even here. People swam, fished.—Every few blocks
the main streets changed names, and the Americans

and American types I met had
given them simpler ones. Neat Street was
tree-lined. Eat Street featured

Nouveau Maxim's.
The main drag was Wilshire. It was on
Beat Street, however,

I met the Communist,
                          three or four days after I arrived.
It wasn't my usual place.

The pleasantness
of downtown, the meditative promenades
of my district were absent. Jazz joints—

great names
with letters missing on the stained marquees;
some rock places

with blackened windows, pink neon signs were
closed when I saw them. People
scuttled here, lurked.

A familiar darkness reigned. Linty sweaters.
Graffiti.—Warehouses, some deceptive. And on corners,
women stood. I wondered

why they would do that
here. Firmly:
they don't want to. Well,

perhaps they are doing it
because they don't want to,
in some sense... Or perhaps

at last
these weren't human beings
but simple functions of another's need.

That lingering doubt
had kept me edgy. Casually
chatting—in shops, on benches—I had acted

a little too bright. But the Communist
struck me as real, as I
set down my plastic bags

on the formica table. (Today, a
Braun coffee grinder, a pound
of Aged Java

for immediate use, several pounds
for the freezer.) It was
the poorest sort of cafe,

not even a picture
or a calendar.
Only the sugar

was white, and the apron
of an Asian woman stacking plates. I don't know
why I decided

to dare this place, or why it felt
daring. He sat amidst newspapers.
His Spanish accent was

only beginning to fade. "I haven't investigated
the papers yet," I said.
                    "They are a nonsense."

He spoke with more passion
than I had encountered here.
                    "Why?"

"News," he spat. "There is no news, no
broadcasts, no wire services, no
communication. They interview newcomers.

Anyway there is no point.
What can we do?" "It's always good
to know, isn't it?" I asked, alarmed.

"It is a torment.
Why 'good'?"
            "Consciousness is always good."

"Conscious of what?" He was
unattractive, hairy and pockmarked, but his eyes
seemed not to know it. I asked

where he was from, what he had done.
He described
the raids that took him

and 3,000 others: the strikes smashed,
the offices of the peasant cooperative
burnt, 10-year-old girls

raped, pregnant women slashed. American
names appeared, ubiquitous
as thorns or wire. He had been

held a long time,
died under torture, said
no more about the torture. Talking

was painful for him, its pointlessness
threatened to stop it. At each point
I urged him on, nervously folding

newspaper. "I
wonder about my friends," he said.
"José Gutierrez, Ramon Blau, El Colombio, La Julia."

"Have you looked them up? There is a
Tracing Office ... gringos, granted,
but nice." He shook his head:

"They are not here.
I hope they are free.
They were not taken when I was." I

saw what he meant,
shuddered; stirred my coffee. "Are you sure that
nothing can be done?" "It is completed,"

he said, and smiled coldly
at something I didn't catch. "Eventually I will go
to see if

those who were poor,
and had no power, and could not help, have at least
comfort. The priest of my village

could not do more."
                          "You could seek out
your torturers, eventually."

                    "That would be pleasant,"
he said, glancing at me. I
couldn't interpret his tone. "Why do you think

this exists, though? You don't seem to
focus on it at all."
He had no answer, except

a weary, fleshy shrug. I
left soon, taking
one of the leftist papers

which in the event
I didn't read. Outside,
an early knife-fight. Bums staggered toward it. On

Beat Street, I learned, some men
got off on dying,
being patched up

and coming back for more. Later that day
my bus
passed that corner, but I

couldn't find the place.
                    Also during that time,
I saw my parents. The Tracing Office

was helpful, within limits; some
names I gave them
weren't listed.—I'd

worried
about running into my
father, unprepared. Had imagined

an art gallery scene.
Marlboro's on Wilshire. I would be
about to move in

on the girl at the desk, and he would
enter like a field marshal,
surrounded by curators,

the art press; point at the paintings, say
"This. That. Not that,"
before he saw me.

Then what. A bear hug. "What are you
doing here?" "Oh, I . . . " "When did you get into town?
Why didn't you call me?"—Or he would

glance at his friends,
then the hug, then
introductions.

Instead I called him.
Visited. He was
tactful, greeted me warmly, asked

nothing I couldn't field.
The apartment
was dark, in rich woods. He had

returned very far:
dark wavy hair, lean tough jaw.
A fedora, wide lapels

would not have been amiss. He
chuckled when I said this; complimented
my own new form.

We looked much alike: not
brothers, perhaps, but
a sergeant and a lieutenant

from the same front, on the same leave.
We talked an hour
about his new collection,

other collections,
museums here. Then we parted,
pledging to keep in touch.

                         My mother had found
an anonymous sort of place
and had not changed. She had "known"

I had died,
        known
what had happened. I had to

talk about it. Stayed
overnight, and another night. I sensed
she had been waiting.

Other older women
lived in the building, she said, and
she had made friends. And the neighborhood

was safe—astonishingly so,
she found, taking
longer and longer walks,

even at night. "Those Government people—is
that what they are? Or are they really angels?"
had been most thoughtful. "Didn't they tell you,"

I asked, "about the . . . power,
the mechanism?" They hadn't.
She hadn't noticed. I felt

absurd, describing it. It was like another boast.
"You can make things
happen, here. You can have anything you want."

She looked doubtful. Yet she had me
in front of her, as testimony. But
although she rejoiced

at how I looked, she wasn't
surprised, somehow. "I can go back, I can
make everything different than it was?"

"No—But you can have things,
here. Better things. Just for the asking.
The wishing."

Hesitantly: "I thought they were going to deliver
my jewels. You know I'm not grasping,
but it took me a long time

to accumulate those few jewels."
"You will have them. You'll find them
in your dresser drawer some morning. Or someone

will bring them. Some young person.
—Just concentrate," I added,
suddenly sure

                they would come
and that she too,
now she had seen me,

though very slowly,
with little consciousness of it,
and no irony,

would go back
to the soft beauty, curls, muted cashmeres
that had been hers. Already she moved more freely,

though unaware of it,
no longer having to fight
that pain.

"I have to go," I said. We embraced, weeping.

                                        Susan
arrived early in April (it was April),

approved of
Neat Street, the house, and
all the furniture

and immediately began to receive
visitors. I recognized them.
Women I had known.

Friends of hers.
One whose moon face
could register no experience, one whose face

had never shown joy. Others. All young,
in the short skirts and turtlenecks of
our youth. They recognized me

but Susan
took them upstairs. I heard
murmuring, sobbing

the silence of
patting. I was on my best behavior,
made coffee,

waited till they descended,
wanting to include me.
                          Thought:

they can't all be dead . . .
                          Then, slowly, realized
Susan's different relation

to time. She was
central. She had called them back
from whatever far

cities and years
they had died in
to the bodies

and problems she remembered. She had called me back
when she was ready
to move. She was never bored

but went on
from triumph to triumph, probably
unable to understand,

if I had mentioned it,
why they were triumphs. Yet I noticed:
the husbands

never appeared. There would be no
handshake, no last analysis,
even prefatory

to eternal parting. When I mentioned this
she pointed out
that I had imagined my parents still

divorced. Also
I was free
(she said with that slow judiciousness)

to bring my (male) friends over.
We could even
find someone for Betty or Sally. It might work.

Why not?
they were "strong" now.
                      Other evenings we read.

Susan continued to pursue
the Library of Alexandria;
burnt by a Christian mob,

lovingly reconstructed
by its scholars. They had awakened—
legend had it—

armed with scrolls and quills.
I was more interested
in writing produced here. Strindberg's *This City*.

Twain's *Our Town*. Pascal's
hundred volumes (he was rumored
still to be at work). I still felt

I was asking the wrong questions. Why were
some names missing? Where were
St. Augustine? St. Paul? (For example.)

(*That* group had
attempted a takeover once,
I gathered—without success: heretics

had winked out
when the flames started to hurt.) Tracking
some of these people down

was one of my two firm plans.—Not just in
literature: I was
sorry not to find

another century of Mozart,
up through the Tristan-chord, encountering,
defining... Where was he? We picked up

Mahler's Eleventh, the "Deliverance,"
at The Discophile, and
the later oeuvre

of Guillaume Lekeu.
                                  I lay on the deep red couch,
she by the fire, listening

to these records
or to the classical station;
the announcer's quiet voice,

his obvious fulfillment.
                                  Rain fell
on the vines. There was spring

and autumn rain. There were seasons—
nothing one couldn't handle,
except in the mountains. There would be snow.

                                  I lay listening
to the safe and quiet city. Sometimes
I was overwhelmed

by the sense of lost wealth found again
in the books we were reading. Until,
tired of these visions

I could barely understand—Strindberg's strange confidence
or the almost voluptuous relief
in the *Reflections* of Hypatia

Susan had put me on to—I
let the book drop,
and, for the first time, thought

of my life as a whole. I could see
the shape of it, it wasn't difficult . . . Then I'd
shrug it off, not

wanting to threaten
this peace. Looking at Susan
gleaming in the firelight, I wondered if

despite her denials
she had summoned
Jack out of futurity—or whether

I was the true end.
                              Then she would
feel my gaze, and gaze at me

and rise and
come over, silk robe trailing,
and say something, in

a husky, smiling voice.
Sometimes one of the "stronger" friends
stayed.

               One morning she made breakfast—
not the usual
bagel and lox, cream cheese, croissant,

cappuccino, orange juice and shirred egg festival we
staged for each other but,
I suspected, a Jack breakfast,

a hubby breakfast. She could tell
I had an errand, beyond my daily
drift round the galleries.

The Palace of Justice
rose from a wooded island
where the river curved through the Southpark.

Majestic bridges
carried "Heat Street"
to it and away.

The Palace was tall,
open, louvred . . . busy: a diamond-
checkerboard effect, with terraces,

helicopter platforms many stories up. It wasn't
the Palace of Justice I'd imagined, but then
one has no clear idea. Beyond the vaulted lobby

with Rivera's mural I
found no centralized Renshawe,
only corridors

and a young man
(though his youth
looked strange, sharp-edged,

something reclaimed in rage. I wondered if
I looked like that).
                    He was carrying papers,

had access to files,
the computer,
computer techs. The harsh light

of the great diamond windows (was this
Melnikov's design?
it had to be) disoriented me. "I—

where should I—
I didn't expect this," l announced. He
welcomed the chance

to strike an attitude. "What *did* you expect?
A solemn temple?
A row of bald heads? God?" "Yes,"

I said simply, "I thought He'd do something
obvious for a change.
I'd open a door,

an ordinary door,
and there he'd be."
                          "With what?"

"An accounting."
                He started to hurry
along the corridor. I kept up. "Of course I

had to leave that part blank," I babbled.
"What he'd say. Otherwise
I'd be imposing it."—He,

coldly: "You're confusing
justice with something else. Justice
doesn't require imagination. Or

influential contacts. It has to be
there for the asking.
Without ambiguity."

                        We reached an elevator,
descended. His lips, his gaze
were pinched, fierce in

righteousness. "And is it
so readily available?" I asked.
He grinned tightly. "The computer has it all.

Did you ever wonder
what people said behind your back? What *women* said?
What various files contained? I don't know

if there were hidden cameras, or whether
it's all a reconstruction
but it's on file here and I'm

preparing my case."
                                        "But,"
I stammered. "Once your

'case' is prepared,
is there a Judge?
A trial?" We entered

another corridor. Here of course
there was no natural light,
but a diamond screen

at the black hallway's end, white numbers on black doors.
He was answering my question,
I realized, and

answering it with contempt. A jagged silhouette
in that light, he led me
a few doors down, said: "When I'm ready

I will come here"
and left. The light buzzed. I knew
what was behind those doors.—I haven't

come very far,
I thought, since "the General" etc.,
                              except

this time I knew
                         The Waffen-SS
was behind this door. And in

the next room
perhaps, its leadership.
And Haig and Westmoreland,

Duvalier and Somoza. And so on. O.K. But
smaller talents, too: that whole
crowd from my past . . . a comparable crowd,

no doubt, of Susan's.
My Ex, her Current,
and every bitch who ever turned me down

also hung
securely from big Xs . . . And by the door,
a sign-in sheet on a clipboard

and all the tools I'd need.
My head throbbed. I hadn't wanted
this kind of personal responsibility. Wondered

why it had reappeared.
Wished that
someone who'd really suffered—some old

Dachau grad holding his skull fragments
from the decompression experiments,
or his testicles

from that sterilization number would come along
to set an example
one way or another.

When I reached home
Susan wanted to talk. We went to a small place on Eat Street.
Showering, dressing up

calmed me.
                She looked lovely
in a lace-topped blue thing

I hadn't seen before,
leaving her shoulders bare.
I wore my tails and cummerbund.

Her face glowed
with wine and candlelight. We talked about nothing,
idly and happily.

About the books, the dead past.
                        "Dear,"
she said—in that quiet way

as if I were dear simply,
absolutely,
                "I want a child."

"You're mad," I said.
Her face changed, and I
again confronted loss. "Can you find

one real objection?" she mourned.
"It would vanish into *space*,
Susan—" I burst out,

then looked for
something that could mean. "The wish-fulfillment
mechanism—you know

what I mean, Susan, you do it in your way,
I in mine,
    but a child,

an infant couldn't
shape it, couldn't restrain it; he'll flicker out
as soon as he emerges, into an

alternate universe of pure tit—
he'll attach himself
to that . . . stupid blue *wall* up there as if it were

another uterus and grow
backwards." "That's nonsense,"
she snapped. "They aren't like that.

He'll want to grow. To
see me. To love."
    "There are no children," I said.

"There are." She stared. "You haven't noticed."
I hadn't.
Now I did. "You only notice yourself,"

she said, without anger.—"That's true. Including
that subtle aspect of myself which seems
alien." "Dear, I didn't mean—" "Why, Susan?

Why this? Is it a fulfillment? . . . Maybe for those
mustached creatures I saw outside
the City, who can't imagine

any other heaven, or maybe someone
who was barren in life—" "But I was barren."
She was weeping now.

"Maybe not in that sense, but I
was barren. I want to have your child.
Is that so bad? It would be marvelous—it

wouldn't be born to die,
to be trammeled, to be
frightened. Anyway, what is

'fulfillment'? Can you imagine it?
I can't. But this is something to do.
Aren't you bored yet?"

                        "No," I said.
I wanted to hurt her,
to grind her under my heel—to hang her

from a steel cross
in that infinite cave beneath our Cave.
"As far as I'm concerned

sex only comes into its own
once it's freed of
irrelevancies." But she saw

through this; smiled, her eyes glimmering.
"It wouldn't diminish
my love for you." "It would, though,

insofar as
it wasn't my idea." "What do *you* want?"
she asked, losing interest. "I was hoping

to love you—" I said, arming myself
with cold against
abandonment. Realizing,

gradually, that I was
waiting for the check.   After that scene

we were unhappy. I didn't die
for this, I joked with myself,
the house no longer

safe... No quarrels, but
a politeness
in her sweetness, a different quality

to the visits—the whispers and laughter
behind her closed doors.
She was drawing in

people and interests
before leaving for
her special place. For the first time

here, I banked up anger.
Settled into it
almost gratefully, thinking: now I would learn the truth.

                    I began to penetrate
the grid of downtown.
I believe I returned

to the lower reaches of Beat Street; the all-night places
where the slobs
died and rose and died,

where the teeny-boppers
sliced up in
girl-gang fights or smashed on motorcycles

arrived still boogying. They affected
scars, graverot,
kept their last wounds. I

danced
since they had
essentially no language. I

fought but was not hurt.—Worked
at converting the penis
to a voluntary muscle. Watched

sadness fall beneath
the superb machine
my will had become.

                Eventually I reached the harbor.
The vast mouth
of the river was filled

with cranes and buoys,
docks, wonderful seaplanes
and ships

arriving and departing
at all hours. Much oil slick. It was
hard to see the sea.

One had to
walk far out on a pier
among the fishermen, or climb to the balcony

of an export-import firm and wait
for twilight. Turning back,
one saw the City

rising away, unimaginably vast:
the lights of Wilshire
and Eat Street, Heat Street, Beat Street, various walls,

the freeways, red
taillights of outbound cars. Meanwhile,
occluding the horizon

from whence they came,
                              ships
full of new arrivals. These were

marvelous old liners
with that Thirties-fantasy air,
like the seaplanes massively sporting.

The dead thronged the rails,
out of their minds with excitement,
laughing and pointing, rousing

the occasional brooder, holding
babies up to look. They were
yellow and brown and black

predominantly, many
in strange rich garb. Already their trip had lasted
long enough for them to change.

Whites among them
chatted, making friends fast. And they debarked
and were welcomed to the City

by drums and tubas, gongs, big flourishes
from gamelan orchestras. Only at dusk
came a break, before

the first night docking (light-
bedecked, with mariachi bands,
candy skulls). The water

turning then
the color of the sky
without a single wave, was, I thought,

water as it is
in itself, water's idea of water,
untouched by outside influences. And I thought:

it isn't the sun I miss
but the moon. It
mattered.—The twilight,

prolonged almost indefinitely,
was a Rothko, broken only by
other watchers, leaning on the railings.

Like me they were
the quiet type,
the type that gathers

where the river meets the sea.

                                        I wasn't home
when she left. I'd begun to haunt

Wolf's Tavern, a place in the harbor.
Dark, low-ceilinged,
a view of some girders.

I don't know
why I chose this place. Few women came,
none looking.

I thought I would sit here
and just be. Let things come to me.
It worked for her.

The women
tended to be delicate,
in shapeless raincoats; added

only a faint perfume
to the smell
of harbor and cigars.

Men sat widely separated.
No music played. Wolf occasionally
turned past

sing-song or rapid-fire voices
on the radio, switched off in disgust,
watched

his little Sony but
kept the volume low. " 'Always polite', "
said Gottfried Benn, 1886–1956, doctor and poet.

"That's Wolf's motto, as it was mine."
                              The place filled up
   when Benn came. Students,

   blond, respectful, pursuing their research
   beyond the last possible credit.
   The comfortable second wife

   (suicide by injection, fearing Russians). A
   fawning ex-informer, who
   thrived on Benn's disdain. A grateful patient

   from his days
   combing bombsites with flashlight and hypo.
                                          The circle

   was sometimes reduced to me, but he still
   played to a gallery: "If any of these swine
   give you trouble, just tell me. There is a trauma—

   the literature has identified it—in learning that
   death cures so little, and they tend to
   take it out

   in obsolete ways. All that shit
   about Jews meant nothing to me." I
   sipped my beer, thinking

   I could wipe the floor
   with swine
   without his help. The feeling that

   coming from me
   strength was pushiness, logic stuffiness,
   grief inaudible,

was here too,
as they were here—beefy nondescripts,
glancing at me sideways, grumbling; but

here they were harmless.
                            " 'The presence of my enemies'.
I said. Benn laughed; I

sensed he hadn't understood.
—"So. You were
drawn to the City

by this
hope for an 'Accounting'," said Benn.
"And . . . your second plan?"

I smiled. "I was hoping
'die Meistern zu ehren', to honor my Masters.
Certain select masters.

To pick their brains." "What?"
I explained.—"A delightful phrase!
I would feel honored, except I know

I was a minor taste."
"Well, it doesn't seem so important, now . . .
I was always bookish—In a sense, I'm

still trying to live via reading.
That line you wrote in '43:
'But action means to serve vulgarity'—"

                            "But for
me to say that—" he said, enjoying himself, "a German—
necessarily a 'political illiterate'—

it distresses me deeply
to hear an American,
a natural democrat—especially one so young—"

"I'm not young," I said, uneasily. "I just
fixed myself up."
                    "*Of* course.

All Americans must be young." "Maybe
'all suicides', " I muttered, an old
masochism rising

to help his clumsy efforts.
"Ah, that too!" he said. "You interest me." "What I
still don't understand," I went on, "is how

at the Tracing Office
I couldn't seem to find anyone. Shakespeare.
Mozart. Jackson Pollock. Kafka. Intellectuals I've met

I've bumped into by
chance. Where is everyone?" "There's no mystery
about *that*," he boomed, "they're asleep."

               "Asleep."
"Ja. Wolf, two more!
—Ja, ja. Asleep! There are places

all across the town, rooms
with . . . little signs: 'Ohne Mich', etwas—"
" 'Do Not Disturb', " I suggested.—"That's it.

Perhaps they only mean
to doze an hour, but it goes on
somehow, and they sleep a thousand years—

open their eyes to find
the candle has gone out. Or they sleep deliberately
in the hope of more interesting company.

I sympathize with this, I have never been satisfied
with the company. But I keep myself awake,
and do not

more than is necessary *indulge*
in these creeping rearrangements
the lizard brain effects here." "So that's it,"

I murmured, suddenly aimless.
"What *I* fail to understand," he said
                                        (I forget if

anyone was around
that day, beside the usual hangers-on),
"is what you expected to learn. I approve your

dropping the idea of a Last Judgment—
that is a bêtise
and, if you don't mind my saying so, a Jewish bêtise."

"I do mind," I said.
"I apologize," he said easily. "But merely to
talk to intellectuals.

Intellectuals. Pigs!
I knew them. Claques, cliques and whoring! South-sea tours.
The white touring-cars! The cream step-ins!

Cocaine! And the sanctimony! 'How can you
lend your support to this regime of
gangsters?' Gangsters. What were they? *Thé-dansants* for

Siberian Relief, when the inflation was at
four trillion—"
"Quiet down," I commanded.

He ignored me, frowned.
"Now, I myself
have done little work these last years. And this is

common, after that first posthumous spurt—
in my case quite lyrical and humanistic,
you would approve. But Art here

becomes as . . . arbitrary as anything else. The difference
between what I called the 'world of Expression'
and any other world

fades. I still function
as a doctor, still diagnose:
lordosis, ulcers,

stones, gout—the diseases of too much sitting,
too much sitting—" (Growl from the regulars, which he
enjoyed.) "Now if one of these fellows

would be kind enough to
have a little heart attack . . ." He
noticed me again. "But I feel no

desire to meet with Goethe. What would I say
to him, or he to me?"
Amused: "You seem to want so much

to be kissed by some Prince,
roused from some sleep of your own . . ."
                                        On other days,

when Benn didn't show up
I
sat without diverson.

                        Why all these krauts?
I wondered ... thought
they had been evil

and beaten
and that seemed
vaguely meaningful.

                    I seemed to have lost
more than Susan.
There was no real

hatred or despair
or speech or even drunkenness
at Wolf's. Each of us

could rise at any time
to seek that special place
listed in the computer.

Was there a resentment
so massive, I wondered, a memory so absorbing
it would stop one from seeking

something that good? My youth and strength,
if nothing else, would have set me apart
from the dandruff, jowls, thick specs, fat little hands

around me,
yet I, too, sat.
                One afternoon, when

the place was empty
(a festival was scheduled,
the Feast of Isis, I believe, on the Esplanade) Wolf

spoke to me, holding
back for a moment
my third schnapps. "I may have

something you're interested in."
                              "Such as?"
"Word from the sleepers."

He grinned. "I was like you, curious. I am
entirely self-educated, you know,
an old Social Democrat.

They aren't
all asleep, despite what Herr Benn says.
Some leave town, some ask

not to be listed. Others . . . no one knows.
But I have films."
"Films." "Films, tapes—" Modestly: "State-of-the-art,

whatever the subject permitted. I was the
first in the City to get into holograms."
                                        "And you have—"

"Quite a collection. I'd appreciate it
if you didn't noise this around."
"No, of course not—" He

pondered, the bland Saxon face sadly
scanning the door for more custom.
"People who dropped in,

over the years . . . One hologram,
especially, might interest you." "This is really
nice of you, Wolf, but

why are you doing it?"
                              "I meet few people
with the proper interest. And then, things

seem to be changing . . . you know." He gestured.
"Up above. This
tavern isn't the spot

it used to be. Despite Herr Benn
or perhaps because of him. I disagree,
just between us, with his nihilism. Though he is

certainly interesting to listen to.
At any event—" He laughed.
I must have looked eager. "We close early tonight

because of the Festival, and I
won't be able to stay. But
come at 11 and

I'll set things up. I believe I can trust you."
I assured him he could. "Who's it of?"
                                    He told me, and I

impatiently killed time
at the house, and at 11
slipped inside

after a few last celebrants
wavered out. Fireworks from the Esplanade,
faint reflections

of sodium arc lamps at the port
lit the tavern eerily. I
sat by the bar,

watching the
table Wolf indicated. The projector
was built into his Sony.

A glow formed. But he
couldn't get the range, and
the projection

failed to intersect. The real table
disconcertingly penetrated
the three men.

                It was a winter afternoon
in the hologram. Beer noises.
Busy shapes—

an arm, a coat,
part of a torso
entered the zone of light, respectfully withdrew.

Wittgenstein was regaling
Freud with
tales of Sirk Corner.

Freud was the
black-bearded, pleasant-eyed
student Charcot knew. ("It would be silly

not to avail oneself," he said later.
"Just to be free of pain
was always the most heartfelt prayer, and

the one that was answered.")
Wittgenstein looked as he always had
until the cancer

took the last thin flesh.
But he had changed
since the last photographs; seemed *gleeful*, camping about

with multivectored humor.
He described his experiences,
massive repression, rough trade,

the worry and scandal of Cambridge.
Freud seemed amused,
relaxed, unembarrassed,

at one point seeking
clarification of a detail
of Vienna gossip, glancing

apologetically at Marx. " 'De mortuis nil nisi bonum', "
Marx said drily, "but
we can say anything we want." So that

he wouldn't be bored, Wittgenstein switched to
common-room tales,
stories of London at war,

his stint in a factory, what he had seen of
the demise of the Party, the role of Attlee, etc.—Marx
also had returned

to the chubby, stern good looks
of his *Rheinische Zeitung* days.
So they talked, merrily enough,

until Freud said, "To business."
Wittgenstein became
instantly disconsolate, his

head hunched into his shoulders. Marx straightened
his already straight back, Freud
sighed. "We have agreed

on the essential determinism
of mental events. And that they are a part
of the overall determinism of nature."

Marx nodded: "Secondly,
that the formation of neurosis
and that of ideology

obey the same laws: a child's or a whole society's
attempt at evasion."
       "Each is a special case

of the other," said Wittgenstein, with his
new, silly wit. Freud glanced at him.
"Thirdly," he said,

"that what matters
is not abstract melding
of two systems... The miner

hearing the cheap timbers groan
the moment before collapsing; the soldier
awaiting the order to fire

at the wrong person—"
       "The bourgeois youth,"
said Marx quietly,

almost inaudibly
over the tavern noise, "his
capacity for love dispersed,

settling at his new desk . . . the once-beautiful skeleton
lying in hospital, refusing food, tearing
the needle from her arm, the lonely old man

unable even to remember
anger—"
         ". . . would not benefit thereby,"

Freud finished.
"Fourth,
that what matters

is not to be decided
here, by us. Here, where there is
nothing to be won

or lost.
And we are on record
as resenting the obscure exigency

that draws us on." Marx
again nodded, impassive; drew
his coat over his shoulders. "Here I must break in,"

said Wittgenstein. "You're moralizing,
not thinking." "On the contrary," said Freud, signalling
Wolf for *his* coat, "it is because

no morality is possible
here, that there is also
no need to talk."

                    "But you can't just shrug off
the fact of our continued consciousness.
Doesn't your doing so

itself bespeak a fixation? Just
possibly, this is
a stage in maturation

and its responsibilities,
however obscure, are real." "Possibly,"
said Freud.

Marx had already moved,
hands clasped behind his back,
out of the zone of light.

"Yet a principle is lacking
to let one know
the difference between caring and not caring,

bearing these responsibilities or not. Anyway
you're faking your concern
for maturity. I know your theory. You're

still playing the mystic. You want to
possess the living,
to reenter the world by

a kind of vampirism."
He stood. Wittgenstein
smiled and shook his head

like one who expects
not to be listened to.
                            "We are not dead," he said.

The hologram ended. The light
died, the two tables became one.
I could smell

the harbor, and
the hot plastic of the Sony. Slowly
my eyes readjusted to the dark.

Firecrackers,
music and cheering
from the Esplanade; the foghorns.

I was alone.

3

One day I walked out.
Simply left everything.

                        She wouldn't return.
Someone would come
to take back the furnishings

or someone
with similar tastes
would move in.

                                   It was time,
I thought, to find that "heavenly mansion"
people had spoken of—I more than most.

Mine would come,
I knew, fully furnished
with the most interesting books,

deep couches, subtle prints.
I would walk in and feel
at home. No need to shop.

No shops nearby. On the desk,
papers
with my writing on them

that I could pick up in mid-thought
and carry on to victory.
So I walked out.

The staff at the
Tracing Office were nice, as always.
They gave me general directions

and a rather medieval map.
Six days' ride north.
The confluence of two

tributaries of the river.
Mountains. It was that vague.
I was nonplussed

at first, but didn't mind:
in the future
I had imagined once, when one arrived

on a new planet,
the city around the spaceport
would be orderly, and one could find one's way

easily, but leaving the city
one would leave
numbers, fixed addresses, any law

but what glance and handclasp might suggest.
This would be different, of course,
from that early fantasy. There would be no stars,

no marvelous alien stars,
whorls and smudges of stars,
so near one could wave at them, or invent

one's own constellations . . . my thoughts
ran on this, as
my bus crossed town.

I found Juggernaut
by the outermost city wall,
cropping the weeds

beneath the gargoyle fountains. One saw
interesting things here: temples
to the unknown god, worn-away

inscriptions.
—Graffiti: the circled A,
any number of swastikas, the Guttering Candle

(the current Gnostic sign,
Susan had told me).
                      I didn't stay.

We rode north,
keeping to the parks, the roadside.
Children

played among the fountains,
learned how to use
swings. I noticed one child, peculiarly

thoughtful, standing apart, with
adults around him. They are
coaxing him to forget

pain, I thought. And there were
merry-go-rounds, hot-dog stands, trashcans.
From the first rise

I looked back
at the towers of downtown.
Over the rise

we lost the highway.
The land opened.
Seagulls wheeled overhead. I

had always liked
birds of the open sea,
scavenging far inland.

I had wondered
what the north end
of the City would be like.

The Los Angeles motif
culminated in vulgar
mansions on hilltops.

Then it was
            already
my land in some sense: small woods

giving promise of forests, dwindling
paths. No
cars would come here, no developers.

                              I was trying
as I rode
to withdraw my attention

from things around me. I would see
where they went
without my support.

It was difficult.
              But by evening
of the third day, I noticed a change:

the land had become
more bare.
Brown rock. Pale trees. Juggernaut found

little to lick and eat.
The distant mountains
stood in dirty haze.

Low, dull scrub.
                Lizards scurried.
Stunted creatures

eyed us from hiding.
I was sad:
I had loved animals,

had been one, here; now
wondered what that had meant.
                        A chill

wind rose.
Juggernaut snorted. I
drew my cloak around me, felt

hungry. Had
packed too few provisions.
Ignored hunger.

It stopped.
Mutated-looking animals
watched us.

We skirted them, entered
a plain of cracked mud,
damp in spots.

Dusk. Silence.
A light source
off to the right. Some

wayside religious thing?
Even that
accounting I had wanted.

I kept going. Like
Kierkegaard, I wouldn't
swerve from my path.

                        The light,
always so diffuse,
thinned, and

absolute darkness came
in stages, as if improvising.
                                  Yet I should have

romped through the cities, smashing
buildings aside with my paws, cars
dripping from my jaws,

ripping streets out with my fangs,
leaping on crowds, then falling
back on my haunches to howl ...

                                 Juggernaut's hooves
raised no sound, only dust.
This dust

seemed insufficiently impersonal—residually
structured, as if
fallen from some catastrophe.

The darkness had changed.
I looked up. Great
rents had appeared

in the surface of the earth
and as we
moved slowly under

one vast opening
I saw the stars.
                    Not the remembered few,

but all that can be seen
without air.
Those long dead,

those being born as I watched,
shone without twinkling.
I had been very cold.

They warmed me.
I felt at last
I lacked for nothing.

The memory of
the Countess' machine
faded.

          Yet
I thought
there may be

other worlds, other
intelligences . . . tentacles
waving from warm muck, chitinous song

of a supernal beauty, words
written in methane.
Other cities.

Beings who even now
regarded each other through
whatever inadequate sense.

Beings for whom
the difficult pronoun
had meaning.

For them one could feel
kinship.
           I blessed them in my heart.

—Maybe, with work,
I could arrange
a trip.

Yet what good would it do
to walk strange streets
invisibly?

Dead, could I talk
only with their dead,
comparing mourning?

Perhaps I would be
different there: substantial—

Biographical Note

Frederick Pollack is the author of two book-length narrative poems—*The Adventure* (Story Line Press, 1986), and *Happiness* (Story Line Press, 1998)—and two collections—*A Poverty of Words* (Prolific Press, 2015) and *Landscape with Mutant* (Smokestack Books, UK, 2018). In print, Pollack's work has appeared in *Hudson Review, Salmagundi, Poetry Salzburg Review, Manhattan Review, Skidrow Penthouse, Main Street Rag, Miramar, Chicago Quarterly Review,* the *Fish Anthology* (Ireland), *Poetry Quarterly Review, Magma* (UK), *Neon* (UK), *Orbis* (UK), *Armarolla, December,* and elsewhere. Online, his poems have appeared in *Big Bridge, Diagram, BlazeVox, Mudlark, Occupoetry, Faircloth Review, Triggerfish, Big Pond Rumours* (Canada), *Misfit,* and elsewhere. His poem "Shelter" won a Princemere Poetry Award in January 2020. Pollack lives in Washington, DC.

www.ingramcontent.com/pod-product-compliance
Lightning Source LLC
Chambersburg PA
CBHW030856170426
43193CB00009BA/627